# Preaching Through the Bible

## Luke 12–24

### Michael Eaton

**Sovereign World**

Sovereign World
PO Box 777
Tonbridge
Kent, TN11 0ZS
England

*By the same author*:
*Genesis 1–11* (Preaching Through the Bible) – Sovereign World
*Genesis 12–23* (Preaching Through the Bible) – Sovereign World
*Genesis 24–50* (Preaching Through the Bible) – Sovereign World
*Applying God's Law* (Exodus 19–24) – Paternoster
*Joshua* (Preaching Through the Bible) – Sovereign World
*1 Samuel* (Preaching Through the Bible) – Sovereign World
*2 Samuel* (Preaching Through the Bible) – Sovereign World
*1 Kings* (Preaching Through the Bible) – Sovereign World
*Ecclesiastes* (Tyndale Commentary) – IVP
*Hosea* (Focus on the Bible) – Christian Focus
*Joel and Amos* (Preaching Through the Bible) – Sovereign World
*The Way That Leads to Life* (Matthew 5–7) – Christian Focus
*Mark* (Preaching Through the Bible) – Sovereign World
*Return to Glory* (Romans 3:22– 5:21) – Paternoster
*Living Under Grace* (Romans 6–7) – Paternoster
*1 Corinthians 1–9* (Preaching Through the Bible) – Sovereign World
*1, 2 Thessalonians* (Preaching Through the Bible) – Sovereign World
*2 Timothy* (Preaching Through the Bible) – Sovereign World
*1 Peter* (Preaching Through the Bible) – Sovereign World
*1, 2, 3 John* (Focus on the Bible) – Christian Focus
*Living A Godly Life* (Theology for Beginners) – Paternoster
*Enjoying God's Worldwide Church* (Theology for Beginners) – Paternoster
*No Condemnation* – IVCP (USA)
*Experiencing God* (Theology for Beginners) – Paternoster

ISBN: 1 85240 283 0


Typeset by CRB Associates, Reepham, Norfolk
Printed in England by Clays Ltd, St Ives plc.

# Preface

There is need of a series of biblical expositions which are especially appropriate for English-speaking people throughout the world. Such expositions need to be laid out in such a way that they will be useful to those who like to have their material or (if they are preachers) to put across their material in clear points. They need to avoid difficult vocabulary and advanced grammatical structures. They need to avoid European or North American illustrations. *Preaching Through the Bible* seeks to meet such a need. Although intended for an international audience I have no doubt that their simplicity will be of interest to many first-language speakers of English as well. These expositions are based upon the Hebrew and Greek texts. The New American Standard Version and the New International Version of the Bible are recommended for the reader but at times the expositor will simply translate the Hebrew or Greek himself.

It is not our purpose to deal with minute exegetical detail, although the commentator has to do work of this nature as part of his preliminary preparation. But just as a housewife likes to serve a good meal rather than display her pots and pans, so we are concerned with the 'good meal' of Scripture, rather than the 'pots and pans' of dictionaries, disputed interpretations and the like. Only occasionally will such matters have to be discussed. Similarly matters of 'introduction' receive only as much attention as is necessary for the exposition to be clear. Although on the surface written simply

3

these expositions aim at a high level of scholarship, and attempt to put the theological and practical message of each book of the Bible in a clear and practical manner. On occasions a simple outline of some 'introductory' matters will be included, perhaps in an appendix, but the first chapter of each exposition gets into the message of Scripture as speedily as possible.

*Michael A. Eaton*

# Contents

## Contents

# Author's Preface

This is of course a very compressed exposition of Luke's Gospel. Preachers who want more of the basic data that is assumed in this exposition may find what they need in the critical commentaries. I.H. Marshall's commentary is perhaps the best on the Greek text. Other works by J.A. Fitzmeyer (a liberal Roman Catholic), John Nolland, Earle Ellis, Leon Morris and N. Geldenhuys are valuable. Expositors will value the commentaries by William Hendriksen and by J.C. Ryle (*Expository Thoughts...: Luke*). Michael Wilcock's exposition is good but he was suffering from lack of space – as I was myself in writing this work! Luke's writings are the longest in the New Testament. The work on the Greek text by J.M. Creed is dated but still valuable. Even more dated is A. Plummer's work in the *International Critical Commentary* – but Plummer's *Cambridge Greek Testament* commentary on Luke is handy for carrying around and using at odd times. There are many more, but these may be top of the list. Joel Green's commentary may be recommended although my own work was done before it was available to me.

This second volume of my preaching on Luke's Gospel continues much along the same lines of the first one, and what I said there applies again. Readers interested in reading all four gospels side by side to get a picture of as much as we know of the life of Jesus should pay special attention to the paragraphs which outline the way the four gospels are moving through the story of Jesus. Many of these messages were preached to the 'University Church' of Chrisco Fellowship which was meeting in the University of Nairobi '8-4-4' lecture theatre, and is led by Pastor Walter Wojiambo and his wife Grace. It is one of my favourite churches in which to preach. I am grateful to the '8-4-4' congregation for their attentiveness. We have had good times together! I am grateful also to family and friends for their help, in different ways, in my work of seeing my preaching into print. Our prayer is that our little book may help preachers.

*Michael A. Eaton*

# Chapter 1

## Fearless Faith

### (Luke 12:1–12)

When we turn to the middle pages of Luke's Gospel and start reading we find that Jesus is travelling towards Jerusalem.

The ministry of Jesus had various phases in it. After Jesus' baptism and a visit to Capernaum, there was **His early Judean ministry**, perhaps during April–December AD 30 (or possibly the dates I mention might all be three years earlier). At the end of this period, John the Baptist was arrested and this led Jesus to make Galilee the centre of His work. It must have begun in early AD 31. A **first phase of Galilean ministry** is related in the events of Luke 4:14–6:11 (the period is more clearly defined in Mark 1:14–3:6). Then in summer AD 31 there was **a second phase of Galilean ministry**. Jesus withdrew to the seaside area of Galilee for a while and then resumed His work from His borrowed home in Capernaum (Mark 3:7–6:6a; Luke 6:12–8:56). A **third phase** of His work in Galilee took place from about early AD 32 to Passover AD 32. It is covered by Mark 6:5b–7:23 and Luke 9:1–17. After this time, Mark tells us of a **period of evading Herod and the Pharisees**. Jesus was constantly on the move so as to elude capture by His enemies. Mark 7:24–8:26 tells the story though Luke says little about it.

Then there came a turning point at Caesarea Philippi (Mark 8:27–30; Luke 9:18–21) when the disciples spoke of their faith in Jesus' Messiahship. At that time Jesus began to give special teaching to His disciples. Mark 8:31–9:50 and Luke 9:22–50 run parallel to each other.

At Luke 9:51 **Luke's travel narrative** begins with Jesus' decision to go to Jerusalem (9:51). He starts travelling towards the city where He knows He will die. On the way He enters a Samaritan village but they reject Him because they hear He is going to Jerusalem (9:52–56). He talks about what it means to follow Him; Luke tells the story of the eager follower and the reluctant follower (9:57–62). The seventy preachers are commissioned (10:1–12). Judgement is pronounced on the Galilean cities (10:13–16). The seventy return (10:17–20). Jesus gives thanks to the Father (10:21–24), answers a scribe's question (10:25–28), tells the parable of the good Samaritan (10:29–37), enters the home of Mary and Martha (10:38–42), gives teaching about prayer (11:1–13), replies to the accusation that His ministry is demonic (11:14–26), tells of true blessedness (11:27–28) and of the 'sign of Jonah' (11:29–32), gives a parable about lighting a lamp (11:33) and the healthy eye (11:34–36). He speaks about Pharisaic inconsistency (11:37–54), and warns against the leaven of the Pharisees (12:1).

This is the point we have reached as we open the pages of the Bible at Luke 12:1. Jesus is on a journey to Jerusalem. At one moment He is clearly in Bethany near Jerusalem. At another moment He seems far from Jerusalem. Evidently there was a lot of wandering around (and Luke may have some stories out of order, rearranging them for his own reasons). Yet the goal in view is Jerusalem.

It is less than a year until the time when Jesus will be crucified. Thousands of people are now following Jesus eagerly, wanting to hear from Him and experience His miracles (12:1a). The current religion of the day is largely hypocritical (12:1b). The Pharisees and their followers make a great display of religion but within they have no knowledge of God.

1. **The secrets of the heart will soon be made known** (12:2–3). Everything hidden will soon be revealed (12:2). Our secret talk will soon be made known (12:3). Every word we have said is recorded and will one day be publicised widely. The Pharisees were secretly plotting against Jesus, but in God's judgement, it will all be revealed (12:3).

2. **The disciples must be fearless** (12:4–5). The Pharisees had a lot of power, and people tended to be afraid of them. But

men can only kill the body (12:4). The anger of God is greater. The body will be raised and there is a resurrection to condemnation and a second death.

It is the anger of God against sin that must be feared and nothing else. There is such a thing as the anger of God against sin. There is the chastening in this life of God's children who displease Him. Zechariah was rebuked for unbelief, and lost some of the joy at the prospect of having a son (Luke 1:20). There is judgement that falls upon the judgmental (6:37). Those who do not respond to the kingdom shall be chastened by a lessening of their experience of the kingdom (8:18). Even what they think they have will be taken away.

There is also the experience of God's wrath by the unsaved in this life. In Luke's version of the Sermon on the Mount Jesus predicts misery for the arrogant rich (6:24), the well fed (6:25a), the person who has no worldly cares (6:25b), the person who is careful to please everyone (6:26). Jesus predicts that the spiritually blind will 'stumble into a ditch' (6:39). Jesus may allow sin to punish itself as when the Gerasenes lost their pigs (8:32–33) and lost His presence as well (8:37), or when villages lose the Word of God because of their unresponsiveness (9:5; 10:11). Self-centred protection of one's life leads to its loss, said Jesus (9:24). Refusal to have Jesus in one's life leads to the last state of the sinner being worse than the first (11:26). Persecutors will suffer God's retribution in this world, even before the final day of judgement (11:50).

Here in Luke 12:5 Jesus speaks also of a future experience of the wrath of God against sin. If the disciples know of the judgement that is coming upon the lost and are conscious of the seriousness of the day when they will have to give an account of how they have lived – then they will fear God and will fear nothing else.

# Chapter 2

# Persecutors and Promises
## (Luke 12:5–12)

The disciples must fear no one because instead of fearing people they are to respect the anger of God against sin. *'I will show you the One you are to fear. Fear him who after the killing has authority to throw into the Gehenna ... Fear him'* (12:5)! Jesus speaks of a future experience of the wrath of God against sin. John the Baptist had used the pictures of useless trees being burned up (3:9), and of chaff being purged out of a granary with irresistible fire that cannot be extinguished (3:17). Jesus had used the picture of a house that collapses into ruins on a day when it is tested by wind and storm (6:48) and had spoken of how 'in that day' it would be more tolerable for Sodom than for some of the towns of Galilee (10:12–15). The punishment of wickedness is a matter of being 'brought down to Hades' (10:15). The generation contemporary with Jesus will be condemned in the judgement, says Jesus (11:29–32). Secret sin will soon be exposed (12:2–3).

The disciples are not to fear those who can kill the body but cannot do anything more than that; rather they are to fear God who can destroy body and soul in Gehenna. Persecutors can snuff out the life of the body in this world, but they cannot extinguish the life of the soul. God can see that sin is thoroughly paid for, and can 'destroy' (Matthew 10:28) the soul.

The Greek word *Gehenna* is the most important of the words for 'hell'. It is used twelve times in the New Testament (Matthew 5:22, 29, 30; 10:28; 18:9; 23:15, 33; Mark 9:43, 45, 47; Luke 12:5 and James 3:6) and always denotes a place of punishment. Gehenna is 'hell' either as the place for the punishment of the devil (James 3:6, which seems to use 'Gehenna' as the devil's home), or as the place where Christians are severely chastised and 'taste' hell (Matthew 5:22, 29, 30; 18:9; Mark 9:43, 45, 47), or where those who reject Jesus are eternally destroyed (Matthew 23:15, 33). The word can be used in a setting where sinners and saints are warned at the same time (Matthew 10:28) and that seems to be the case here also (Luke 12:5). 'Gehenna' is also the term used in connection with punishment after the resurrection. Punishment **before** the day of resurrection is a reality (see Luke 16:23) but in this connection 'Gehenna' is not used.

1. Despite the opposition of traditional religion, **the disciples must be quite confident in God**. God cares for sparrows; He will surely care for human beings (12:6). He has intimate knowledge and concern over every aspect of our lives (12:7).

2. Despite the opposition of traditional religion, **the disciples must always acknowledge Jesus boldly** (12:8–9). If they openly speak of their faith in Jesus, then Jesus will openly speak of them to the Father and before the angels. It is generally thought this takes place at the judgement day, and rightly so, but there is no reason to restrict it to the judgement day. God openly 'confessed' Job before the angels during his lifetime (Job 1:8). Jesus takes pleasure in us before God when we confess Him. Those who deny Jesus because of their fear of mockery or enmity – and Jesus is speaking to disciples (12:1) – will suffer loss in the day when Jesus presents His people to the Father.

3. Jesus still has the opposition of the Pharisees in mind when He warns that **rejection of Jesus is unforgivable** (12:10). The Spirit often worked with great power when Jesus was ministering to men and women in dependence on His Father. When the Pharisees attributed His power to Satanic help (11:15) they were deliberately rejecting Jesus despite the powerful working of the Holy Spirit. They were 'blaspheming' (slandering, rejecting with scorn) the Spirit's testimony to Jesus as God's Saviour. It was unforgivable because it was rejecting the means of forgiveness. To speak against Jesus out of ignorance is forgivable. Even Saul of Tarsus who blasphemed against Jesus and persecuted Christians (see

1 Timothy 1:12–13) was forgiven. He acted ignorantly in unbelief. But to deny Jesus when there is clear and convincing evidence that Jesus is indeed from God is a different matter. Resisting the Spirit's convicting work is more dangerous than resisting Jesus in ignorance. The latter is forgivable. The former is unforgivable, because it is resisting the way of forgiveness (Jesus Himself presented to us in the power of the Spirit). It ought to be added that the 'blasphemy against the Holy Spirit' is not a sin that a Christian can commit, since it involves deliberate, unbelieving rejection of Jesus.

Everything Jesus says about the Pharisees is sobering and challenging. Much depends on whether we boldly acknowledge that we have confident faith in our Lord Jesus Christ. The Pharisees, although they were religious people, rejected Jesus and fell into a sin which cannot ever be forgiven. The Pharisees were generally unforgiven because their wilful rejection of the Holy Spirit's powerful testimony meant that it never had any impact upon their hearts. No matter how powerfully the Spirit was at work the Pharisees – generally speaking – did not wish to seek the forgiveness of their sins from Jesus.

4. Amidst the opposition the disciples will face, **they will receive the special help of the Holy Spirit**. On occasions they will be brought before their persecutors (12:11) but at such times they need not be anxious. In difficult circumstances a special working of the Spirit is promised, and they will find themselves being given the right words to say (12:12).

People like the Pharisees would become persecutors of any who declared their faith in Jesus, and it was this that led to Jesus' words of challenge and encouragement. The greatest promise of all was the assurance that in agonisingly difficult times the special help of the Holy Spirit would be given.

# Chapter 3

## The Rich Fool

### (Luke 12:13–34)

Jesus is preaching mainly about the Pharisees (see 11:37, 45; 12:1). Suddenly a man shouts out from the crowd. *'Tell my brother to divide the inheritance with me,'* he calls out. While Jesus is preaching, the man is thinking about a family quarrel in which his brother will not release a share of the family wealth. Jesus is speaking about judgement day and the danger of a sin that is eternally unforgiven, but the man in the crowd is thinking about money! People get the idea that the Christian faith is all about making our earthly life easier.

But Jesus answers bluntly. *'Who appointed me a judge or divider over you?'* (12:14). Jesus – and His church – are not here just to make life easier for people. There are many agencies that do that, but Jesus and His people have a bigger calling. The Christian faith is not just a means to prosperity. The preaching of Jesus was mainly concerned about our relationship to God, the forgiveness of our sins, and the willingness of God to relate to us personally and get His will done in our lives. And the Christian faith has a lot to say about reward in heaven. It is concerned about eternal destiny.

But it is amazing how often the gospel gets misunderstood or corrupted. People think – as this man in Luke 12 did – that the Christian church is simply a social agency to solve the world's problems. 'The church likes religion' – so says the world to itself – 'and it uses religion to make life a little more comfortable for us and to pray for us when we are in trouble! If my brother will not pay me the money I am owed – Jesus is just the person I want. He is a kind of general helper to everybody and will help me get my money.' So says the world! But, of course, this is not the main work of Jesus at all. Jesus comes to tell us of sin and salvation. The Christian church has the task of calling men and women to new life by the blood of the Lord Jesus Christ.

So Jesus rebukes the man. 'Who appointed me a judge or divider over you?' 'Who gave me that work?' asks Jesus. 'That is not why I am here at all.'

He goes on to warn the man. *'Take heed of covetousness . . .'* (12:15). And then He tells the 'parable of the rich fool'.

The rich man prided himself (12:16–19) on his intelligence, his success, his efficiency and foresight in doing business. He had plans to ensure his comfort for years to come and was planning a contented retirement for himself. But God calls him a 'fool' (12:20).

1. **He thought he was intelligent**. He felt he was a good businessman, cleverly making arrangements for the success of his business. But what is intelligent about not thinking about the unreliability of life?

2. **He thought he had foresight**. There he was planning the future, being very careful to think about everything long before the time, so that he would not suddenly get into difficulties. He was dreaming about a wonderfully successful future in the years ahead. But his thinking about the future only went as far as a few years. He was not thinking about what lay ahead of this life. He was concerned about old age but not about eternity.

3. **He thought he was successful** but what is successful about a man who dies leaving everything? He thought he was covering every possibility but there was one possibility he was not considering – that his life might not be as long as he expected.

4. **He thought he was in command of the situation**. He would do this, and he would do that! But he was not as much in control as he thought he was. He could not choose how long his life would last.

5. **He was concerned about things and possessions but not about himself and his relationship to God**. He was very concerned about material riches but not about spiritual riches (12:21). He was not 'rich towards God', rich in faith, rich in

concern for the needy, rich in spirituality, rich in concern for the kingdom of God.

No wonder God called him a fool. At the height of his success God decided his life had gone on long enough and it was time to call him to account for the way he had lived.

The incident of the man interrupting Jesus leads Jesus on to talk further about money. Anxiety is needless. (i) Life is bigger than possessions (12:22–23). (ii) God will give what is needed without our striving. The ravens are fed without anxiety; the same God who cares for them will feed His people (12:24). (iii) Worry cannot achieve anything (12:25). Verse 26 (which has no parallel in Matthew[1]) makes the point that since it cannot add the tiniest unit to one's length of life why not simply do what has to be done and leave all the strain to God? (iv) God adequately clothes flowers; He will even more clothe His people (12:27–28). (v) They must be a contrast to godless people (12:29–30a). (vi) They must trust that God knows their needs (12:30b) and (vii) must have their attention elsewhere in seeking the kingdom which God is eager to give them (12:31–32). (viii) They must be generous to others (12:33a) and (ix) lay up reward in heaven (12:33b). (x) The supreme delight of their life – whether it is money or God's kingdom – will captivate their 'heart'. If money is the delight of their life, their hearts will be earthbound. Let them make God and His kingdom to be their precious treasure (12:34).

## Note

1. For fuller exposition of verses like these in Matthew 6, see Michael Eaton, *The Way That Leads to Life: The Sermon on the Mount* (Christian Focus, 1999), pp. 141–158.

# Chapter 4

# Ready for Jesus' Coming

## (Luke 12:35–48)

After the parable of the rich fool Jesus follows up His story with direct teaching in which He urges His disciples to freedom from anxiety (12:22–34), readiness in His service (12:35–40), and to faithfulness (12:41–48).

'This night your life is required of you,' said God to the rich fool. Yet Jesus can visit and summon His people in more than one way. One day Jesus will return to this world bodily. He will come in shining majesty to end the world and bring in the day of judgement. But there are other ways in which Jesus can come. He comes in answer to prayer, in sudden blessings, and sudden judgements.

Whatever form the coming of Jesus may take Jesus warned us to be always ready. **Jesus goes on to speak of watchfulness**. He uses the picture of a house-worker who is ready for his employer to return suddenly.

1. **Let Jesus find us engaged in His service**. *'Let your loins be always girded...'* says Jesus (12:35). He is using picture-language taken from the clothing of the ancient world. Men wore long flowing robes. When they needed to do anything that required action, these were tied up around the waist. 'Let your loins be always girded' means 'Get ready for action'.

2. **Let Jesus find us ready and eager for His arrival**. *'Let your loins be always girded, and your lamps burning'* (12:35). He goes on to put the matter to us in a parable. The master goes away, but he requires his servants to stay awake ready to open the door to him and serve him when he returns (12:36). If they are awake when he comes he will serve them (12:37)! The master may even come after great delay (12:38). His sudden

20

arrival will be like that of a thief (12:39—40). It is surprising to find that the master serves the servant. We expect it to be the other way around. When Jesus finds us faithful He likes to reward us. He enjoys ministering to us and (when we are faithful) He wants to minister to us even more than we minister to Him.

3. **Let Jesus find us faithful**. Peter asks who the intended audience is in the parable that has just been given (12:41, referring to the parable in 12:36—40). Sometimes when we listen to the Word of God we like to think how suitable it is for other people!

There is an important principle of interpretation here. Sometimes Jesus has things to say to His disciples and things to say to outsiders at the same time! The thought of judgement is mainly for the outsiders – and yet it is for the believers as well. The wicked person can be thrown into the fire of eternal hell, but the Christian might also be 'hurt' by the second death. There is such a thing as being saved 'through fire' (1 Corinthians 3:15). Christians have to be just as ready as anyone else because although they do not need to fear eternal punishment and do not need to lack assurance of final salvation – yet loss of reward and salvation 'through fire' is still a fearful thing. It is a fearful thing for even Christians to fall into the hands of the living God. Even an apostle could ask: 'Lord, are you telling this parable to us?' Peter was ready for warnings of sudden judgement for others, but he was surprised that Jesus seemed to be including the apostles as well!

Jesus answers in another parable! He asks a question in return. *'Who is the faithful and wise manager...?'* (12:42). The Christian is like a servant who is left in charge as the manager of a large house. He has freedom and responsibility. Yet from time to time he must give account (12:42—43). If he is faithful the reward will be further responsibility (12:44). But if he is unfaithful he will suffer loss and – although he is not an unbeliever – will share something of the unbelievers' suffering in judgement (12:45—46).

Three sins will be specially dealt with in the day of the master's 'visitation'. (i) **Ill-treatment of others may be suddenly**

**judged** (12:45–46). When the manager gets careless and thinks his master is not likely to arrive just yet, he begins *'to beat the menservants and maidservants'* (12:45). He starts treating other people badly. (ii) **Living for pleasure may be suddenly judged**. The careless manager starts eating and drinking from his master's supplies (12:45). He is more concerned about his pleasures than he is about his responsibilities. If the master arrives suddenly he will face terrible and swift punishment.

(iii) **Sin against knowledge may be suddenly judged** (12:47–48). It is not that an ignorant servant will escape altogether. Even the servant who did not know his master's will gets punished. There are three kinds of person here. There is the person who does not know the master's will and does not do it. He is punished. Ignorance is no excuse. God gives us plenty of ways of knowing His will. There is the person who **does** know the master's will but still does not do it. Then there is the person who knows the master's will and does do it. The second category is the worst. The last category is the only place of safety.

Increase of knowledge results in increase of responsibility. These verses throw some light on the nature of God's wrath. There are degrees of punishment. There is such a thing as salvation through fire. The Christian must set out to pursue the opposite of what Jesus denounces. Instead of ill-treatment he pursues love. Instead of pleasure he pursues discipleship and lets God abundantly pour joys and pleasures upon him of a higher nature altogether. Instead of refusing knowledge or neglecting knowledge, he seeks it and he works it out – and so is ready for the Master to be pleased when He comes.

# Chapter 5

## An Age of Conflict
### (Luke 12:49–59)

Jesus is on a journey to Jerusalem; Luke is telling us of the things that happen as Jesus travels in a roundabout manner towards Jerusalem. On this journey He urges the disciples to constantly maintain a fearless acknowledgement that they belong to Him (12:2–9). He talks of the Holy Spirit (12:10–12) and warns against greed (12:13–34), urging them to be watchful (12:35–48). He warns about division in households (12:49–53), and speaks of interpreting the times (12:54–56) and making agreement with one's accuser (12:57–59).

1. **Jesus corrects the idea that the gospel is designed to make life easier for us**. It seems that what is happening here still goes back to the incident in Luke 12:13. Jesus used the incident when His preaching was interrupted to talk about wealth and greed, and to encourage His disciples to avoid anxiety and to be ever ready in God's work. But His comment in 12:14 also needs development. Jesus has said what He did **not** come to do, but what did He come to do? Luke 12:49 answers the question. Jesus says, *'I have come to bring fire on the earth, and how I wish it were already kindled'* (12:49).

There are a number of sayings of Jesus that begin with the words 'I have come'. These sayings are very helpful because they tell us the purpose of Jesus' coming to this world.

But what does this saying mean? What is the fire? What does fire do? It exterminates and it purifies! It consumes rubbish. Luke has already told us about this. John the Baptist came warning of God's exterminating fire. Fire is often used as a picture of judgement. Luke's references to fire are in 3:9, 16, 17; 9:54; 12:49; 17:29; 22:55. Fire exterminates, wipes out of existence. Rubbish is thrown into fire (3:9). God's fire cannot be put out; it is 'unquenchable' (3:17). It exterminates rubbish. So it 'cleanses' (3:17) by wiping out of existence the dirt (3:17); it 'burns up'. Every reference to 'burning up' in the New Testament (Matthew 3:12; 13:30, 40; Luke 3:17; Acts 19:19; 1 Corinthians 3:15; Hebrews 13:11; 2 Peter 3:10; Revelation 8:7; 17:16; 18:8) has the idea of utter extermination. What is burned up eventually 'passes away' (2 Peter 3:10). Jesus comes to bring an end to the reign and rule of sin.

The next saying is: *'I have a baptism to be baptised with ...'*. What sort of 'baptism' is this? It is a baptism of suffering. It has nothing to do with water baptism! We must get rid of the idea that whenever we see the word 'baptism' it is a reference to a ceremony with water!

Jesus is still following up the incident mentioned in 12:13. Jesus did not come to be a social welfare-worker solving disputes about money in families that cannot agree. Jesus came to cast fire upon the earth – to bring in the burning, purifying acts of the kingdom of God! How often people want to use 'religion' – even Christian 'religion' – to make their life easy and help pay the rent! Or to get God's help in solving family finances or in dealing with a greedy brother. But God's kingdom is much more than our little squabbles and anxieties. Jesus comes to destroy sin in a fiery judgement.

Jesus' fiery judgement comes by way of His death upon the cross. He has set His face steadily in the direction of Jerusalem where He knows He will die and be raised again. It is there that He will face His 'baptism', His immersion into suffering.

2. **Jesus is eager to accomplish His life's work**. *'How I am troubled until it is accomplished!'* (12:50). Jesus is not focusing on getting His own life comfortable. He is eager to accomplish something for God.

3. **Jesus is more likely to intensify family conflicts than to settle them**. The man back in Luke 12:13 had wanted Jesus to settle a family dispute and make life easier for him. But Jesus corrects the idea that the gospel is designed to make life easier for us. Has Jesus come simply to help us get money out of our family? No! There are rewards in being saved, but the best of them are after this life. The rewards God gives us in

24

this life are mixed in with hardships and trials. One hardship that might be our destiny is the pain of being separated from people with whom you want to be close. Jesus speaks of 'a family divided against each other'. Maybe in one particular family some are saved; others are not. It creates a division. We wish that division were not there but it is! It does not often happen that an entire family come to salvation. The picture is of a family of five: mother, father, son, daughter, daughter-in-law. But the family is not united since some are supporters of God's kingdom; others are against it.

4. **Jesus asks the crowd to note the signs of the age in which they live**. This age in which we live is an age where divisions of this nature are bound to happen. It is not a time for seeking comfort or defeating a member of our earthly family in some dispute about family wealth.

This age is an age of conflict. Jesus is casting fire upon the earth already! People can interpret the weather (12:54–55), but they are hypocrites and are unable to interpret the time in which they live (12:56). They are unwilling to see this as an age in which God is acting through Jesus. It is an age of division – created by Jesus. It is an age beginning with the suffering and resurrection of Jesus. Why can they not discern that Jesus is bringing in a new epoch in the history of the world? Luke 12:57–59 means 'get right with your fellow men and women before God's judgement falls' (12:57–59). Jesus still has the situation of 12:13 in mind.

# Chapter 6

# Suffering Because of Sin?

(Luke 13:1–9)

We have seen that Jesus made use of an interruption in His preaching (see 12:13); now He makes use of something that had recently happened among the events taking place in Judea. Jesus speaks about things that are of interest to people.

The Roman governor, Pilate, had killed some men while they were sacrificing at the temple. This was typical of Pilate. We know of various times when Pilate killed opponents or trouble-makers. On one occasion he killed three thousand! I suppose there was some kind of rioting in the temple; Pilate sent in his soldiers and a number of people were killed.

Then there was another tragedy. A building in Siloam had collapsed, killing eighteen people. Everyone was talking about these events and Jesus referred to them in His teaching.

1. **Suffering is not a sign of special wickedness**. When tragedies of this kind happen, people tend to think that the suffering person was a great sinner and had deserved special punishment. This was the view of Job's friends (see Job 4:7; 8:20; 22:4–5; compare John 9:1–2). But suffering is not a sign of special wickedness! There are plenty of suffering people who have not specially sinned. And there are plenty of wicked people who are not specially suffering!

2. **People like to interpret what is happening in the lives of others, but not in their own lives**. It is obvious that these events were much discussed in Judea. Everyone was debating the details of how these people in Jerusalem and at Siloam were killed. Why did it happen? Was it because they had specially sinned? Hundreds of people were interested in knowing what had happened and why it had happened. Yet the very people

who like to interpret what is happening in other people's tragedies do not do much thinking about what is likely to happen to them! What might God do to them? What sudden calamity could fall upon them? Are they living in such a way that they have an unblemished record and can feel confident that no disaster will fall upon them? People like to think that others are being punished for their sins, but they also like to think that their own sins will somehow go unpunished!

Don't make the suffering of the other person even worse by your 'interpreting' his tragedy in this way. Don't say to him or to his family, 'If you were more righteous you would not be suffering...'. Don't be a 'Job's comforter'. When you think a person is suffering because of his sins, you are adding to his sufferings – or to the sufferings of those who are bereaved.

3. **God is totally free in the way in which He brings life to an end**. These people in Jerusalem and at Siloam were suddenly removed from this life. Others were allowed to live much longer. Sudden disaster is not punishment of those who have died; it is a warning to those who are alive. Unless you repent, you will perish. The word 'perish' here means 'die suddenly while unreconciled to God'. One day we will die – maybe suddenly, maybe not so suddenly. But unless we have repented of our sins, our death will be 'perishing'. It will be dying without being reconciled to God – and therefore facing God's anger against sin.

4. **Every sudden event is a call to repentance – and especially repentance for our unfruitfulness**. The people gossiping about the recent events need themselves to repent – to entirely change their attitude and outlook towards God and towards the godly life. God especially wants fruitfulness. Jesus tells a parable (13:6–9) which is connected to the previous story. A vineyard owner looks for fruitfulness from his vineyard. If it is not fruitful he will re-use the ground for something else. But the vineyard-keeper pleads that the fig-tree be left one more year before it is cut down.

This is a parable about what God is looking for. Jesus is travelling to Jerusalem. What will He find when He gets there? God wants fruitfulness. The people of Jerusalem have been allowed longer to live! Most of them have not been killed by

Pilate. No tower of Siloam has fallen on them. God has given them more time to repent.

We remember that less than forty years after Jesus' ministry, the Roman armies would march upon Jerusalem, besiege it and then destroy it. Jerusalem was given time to repent, but then sudden calamity would come upon the entire city and nation.

The greater the privileges, the greater the response God wants. We are very happy to discuss the tragedies of others' lives and wonder why events have overtaken them. But we too will sooner or later find that events will overtake us. We are always taken by surprise at the big events that happen in our lives.

Has someone you know suddenly been called away from this life? He or she has had to give an account to God of how he or she has lived. It is appointed for people once to die – and afterwards comes the judgement (Hebrews 9:27). What happened to them is a call to you to be ready at all times to give an account of your life to God.

Are you suffering? It does not mean that God is specially punishing you. He is not taking His revenge against you. God punished sin upon the cross! Jesus has already been punished for your sins! What God wants from you more than anything is fruitfulness. He wants some kind of reward for the time and trouble He has invested in you. He is still allowing you to live; He hopes you will become fruitful. Meanwhile God is being greatly merciful to you; He is allowing you longer to live.

# Chapter 7

# A Word and a Touch

## (Luke 13:10–17)

Jesus was teaching in a synagogue on a Saturday, that is, on the Sabbath day (13:10). Among the worshippers there was a woman who had been attacked by an evil spirit and, as a result, had been a cripple for eighteen years (13:11). Jesus heals her (13:12–13) but the synagogue leader criticises the people for coming to be healed on a Sabbath (13:14). Jesus replies to the man (13:15–16). The critics are silenced but the common people are happy (13:17).

There seem to be thirty-five miracle stories in the gospels. Twenty-six of them are healing miracles or exorcisms.[1] Jesus has supreme authority, because He was (and still is, in heaven) a man of perfect faith. The miracles are proofs of His faith. They are also illustrations of spiritual experiences. The ease of Jesus' miracles illustrates the ease with which He can forgive (see Mark 2:1–17). The power He has over the body is a sign of the power He has over our relationship to God. Deafness is parallel to spiritual deafness, blindness to spiritual blindness, and so on. The miracles are indications of Jesus' lordship over creation, over Satan, over disease and over death. They are foretastes of heaven, and often foretastes of the resurrection body. They are examples of what He might in His sovereignty do for us. God has total freedom in when and how He gives miracles. He is sovereign in His giving faith for miracles. Sometimes – and the story in Luke 13:10–17 seems to be an example – He works a miracle without being asked. He does it just because He wants to! Miracles cannot be 'switched on' just when we like; but our God still works sovereignly to minister to men and women in need.

29

1. We see **a woman whose religion had brought her no relief**.
Jesus calls her a 'daughter of Abraham' which must mean that
she was a true woman of faith. Can a person be truly saved
and yet be oppressed by Satan for so long? It seems so. A
believer can be 'delivered' in that she is truly in the kingdom
of God, and yet still be vulnerable to Satanic attack. Satan
was not planning to let go of this 'daughter of Abraham'
easily.

Eighteen years! Why had she got no help for eighteen years?
One does not like to say it – but it was the church she went to!
The synagogue leader did not like this woman being healed at
all! He was legalistic. Jesus is very severe with him, as he is
with religious people who do not like it when others get
blessed by Jesus. 'You hypocrite!' He says.

2. Consider **what she needed**. She needed a liberating word
from Jesus (13:12) and a liberating touch from Jesus (13:13).
She got both. He spoke to her and He touched her.

3. **How then did she come to get this liberating word and
liberating touch from Jesus?** She was faithful in attending a
meeting where Jesus was known to be present. She had been
crippled for many years. One might have thought that a
woman in her condition had good reason not to be in the
synagogue. If anyone had an excuse for staying at home, it
was her. But she was obviously diligent in getting to be where
Jesus was ministering.

4. It is surprising, perhaps, to discover that **church leaders
often do not like people being healed by Jesus**! One would think
the synagogue leader would be delighted to have a woman
who had been distressed for eighteen years, now healed and
released. But the church leader is angry about the whole
business. He held to a legalistic view of the Sabbath. It was a
peculiar idea of keeping a holy day – to forbid God from
doing any good thing on it! Legalism gets itself into peculiar
contradictions at times. Religious people like to have quite
strict rules about quite small things. 'Holy days' were part of
the Mosaic law and religious leaders loved this part of the law,
and even exaggerated it.

However, their strictness was more for others than themselves. If they had an animal that was distressed on the

Sabbath, they would do something about it. They were happy for an animal to be cared for but not a human being! It just shows that legalism gets very hypocritical.

Ordinary people are often full of common sense whereas legalistic church leaders can make very foolish decisions at times. The leader of the synagogue would rather not have God do anything miraculous on a Saturday! But theological theory is of no value if it does not bring spiritual experience. The ordinary people were more practical. The legalistic Sabbath-lovers missed what Jesus was doing. Meanwhile quite ordinary people experienced Jesus' miracles!

## Note

1. Healing an official's son (John 4:46–54); delivering a man with an unclean spirit (Mark 1:21–28; Luke 4:33–37); healing Peter's mother-in-law (Matthew 8:14–15; Mark 1:29–31); cleansing a leper (Matthew 8:2–4; Mark 1:40–45; Luke 5:12–15); healing a paralytic (Matthew 9:1–8; Mark 2:1–12; Luke 5:17–26); the sick man at Bethesda (John 5:1–15); the man with a withered hand (Matthew 12:9–13; Mark 3:1–5; Luke 6:6–11); the centurion's son (Matthew 8:5–13; Luke 7:1–10); the widow's son (Luke 7:11–17); the blind and dumb spirit (Matthew 12:22–32; Luke 11:14–23); the demoniacs at Gadara (Matthew 8:28–34; Mark 5:1–20; Luke 8:26–39); the woman with a haemorrhage (Matthew 9:20–22; Mark 5:25–34; Luke 8:43–48); Jairus' daughter (Matthew 9:18–26; Mark 5:22–43; Luke 8:41–56); two blind men (Matthew 9:27–31); a dumb spirit (Matthew 9:32–34); the Syrophoenician woman's child (Matthew 15:21–28; Mark 7:24–30); the deaf man with a speech impediment (Mark 7:31–37); the blind man of Bethsaida (Mark 8:22–26); the demon in a boy (Matthew 17:14–21; Mark 9:14–29; Luke 9:37–42); a man born blind (John 9:1–7); a woman infirm for eighteen years (Luke 13:10–17); a man with dropsy (Luke 14:1–6); Lazarus (John 11:1–44); ten lepers (Luke 17:11–19); Blind Bartimaeus (Matthew 20:29–34; Mark 10:46–52; Luke 18:35–43; Malchus' ear (Luke 22:49–51). In addition there are at least two places where it says that large numbers of people were healed by Jesus: (i) Matthew 8:16–17; Mark 1:32–34; Luke 4:40–41; (ii) Luke 5:14–16.

# Chapter 8

## The Kingdom of God

(Luke 13:18–21)

The main theme of Jesus' preaching was the kingdom of God. When the angel Gabriel first announced the coming of Jesus, Mary was told, *'the Lord God will give to Him the throne of ... David ... he will reign ...; and of his kingdom there will be no end'* (1:32–33). When Jesus spoke of His preaching, He said, *'I must preach the kingdom of God ...'* (4:43). Luke tells us He preached 'the good news of the kingdom' (8:1). When He sent out His disciples, He told them to 'preach the kingdom of God' (9:2; see also 9:60). Sometimes He would take His disciples aside and speak to them concerning the kingdom of God (9:11). When Jesus preached the Sermon on the Mount – perhaps His greatest preaching – its main theme was the godly life in members of the kingdom of God. 'Yours is the kingdom ...', Jesus said in His opening words (6:20). The 'kingdom of God' took a dramatic step forward when Jesus came into this world. The very least person who experiences the kingdom through Jesus' working in his or her life is greater than John the Baptist who belonged to an earlier stage in the history of salvation (7:28).

The 'kingdom of God' is a phrase that speaks of experiencing the power of Jesus as God's King. Jesus is the King. Where Jesus is, there is the kingdom of God. The kingdom of God is God getting His will done on earth by sending and using King Jesus. The 'royal power of God' sometimes acts in dramatic ways. Luke 9:27 probably refers to the demonstrations of God's power seen in the outpouring of the Spirit and in the fall of Jerusalem.

The parables are an invitation to experience the kingdom of God. Jesus says, *'To you has been given to know the secrets of the kingdom of God'* (8:10). Jesus uses two parables. The kingdom of God is like a mustard seed (13:18–19); and it is like the working of yeast (13:20–21).

1. **The kingdom of God may be compared to a mustard seed** (13:18–19). God's kingdom is not a place; it is an experience. It is not a locality; it is the kingly and royal power of God working within us through Jesus, God's King. The parable of the mustard seed makes the point that the kingdom has small beginnings but leads to big results. The mustard seed was very small, about a millimetre in size, but it grew into something large and strong. The tree that would grow from the seed could be about three metres high or more, and was strong and sturdy. Quite large birds would sometimes perch on its branches.

When God is acting in this world through Jesus, His King, He often acts in a very small way. The world hardly notices what is happening.

People in Jesus' day tended to misunderstand the kingdom. They thought of it mainly in terms of political power and looked for some kind of revolutionary movement that would force the Roman soldiers out of Israel. There were promises in the Old Testament about the kingdom of God being like a mighty tree (Ezekiel 17:22–23; 31:1–14; Daniel 4:11–12).

It is true that the kingdom of God, eventually, produces mighty results. It affects nations and empires, and it does have political results – in the long run. But the kingdom of God does not begin with revolutionary violence. It begins with individual men and women coming to new life by their faith in Jesus. It begins with Jesus driving back the forces of darkness and the power of sin, in the lives of particular people.

Both individually and internationally, the royal power of God tends to act quietly and inconspicuously at first. When Jesus was born, He was born in a stable. He ministered in a despised part of Israel called Galilee. His earliest followers were fishermen and wicked people whose lives had been dramatically changed.

But the quiet beginning led to something gigantic and enormous. It revolutionised people's lives and was destined to change the history of the world.

We should never despise small beginnings in the things of God. Whether it be in world-wide outreach, or whether it is a matter of what God does in our own lives, God has a habit of beginning in a small way!

2. **The kingdom of God may be compared to the working of yeast** (13:20–21). When an Israelite housewife wanted to bake some bread, she would have a little piece of fermented dough – a piece of dough left over from the previous time of cooking and allowed to go sour and slightly alcoholic. She would take a piece of this old left-over dough and mix it with a large quantity of flour. Luke refers to 'three measures', enough to make bread for a hundred people. The effect of the 'leaven' or 'yeast' or 'sour dough' would be to make the entire mass of flour rise and become bread. Without the 'yeast', it would be more like a hard biscuit. Jesus uses this as a picture of the spreading influence of the kingdom of God. It happens in our lives personally, one by one. And it happens internationally, as the influence of changed lives spreads. The kingdom of God may begin in a small way, but then it starts affecting everything. It affects every area of our own lives, and then it starts to affect cities and provinces and countries. Whole nations rise to greatness because of the influence of the royal power of God at work in people's lives. It does not begin with worldly enterprises. It begins with the coming of Jesus into the world, and into our personal life. But then the royal power of God transforms everything. What Jesus does is despised by the world, but what Jesus does will eventually conquer the world.

# Chapter 9

## 'Strive to Enter In'
### (Luke 13:22–35)

One day, Jesus was asked a question, *'Lord, are only a few people going to be saved?'* (13:22–23). It is a wonderful question. How many people – we wonder – will ever get to experience salvation? Will the world ever get to be mainly Christians? How much will the gospel succeed in this world? Jesus spoke of winning the nations, but how successful will we be?

It was a wonderful question – but Jesus never answered it! His reply was: *'Make every effort to enter through the narrow door!'*

1. **Christian teaching is not to become an intellectual hobby in which we discuss interesting questions**. God's church does not go forward through head-knowledge only. People can know the answer to many questions, but yet have little spiritual power. The important thing is to apply what you know. I sometimes get involved in 'question-times' or 'discussion meetings' or 'picking the pastor's brains' (as it was once called!). But I become less and less interested in those kinds of meetings. They seem to me to be entirely useless! Christian teaching is never to become simply a matter of intellectually interesting questions. There will be plenty of good theologians in hell – except that they were not good enough in their theology to ask fewer questions and spend more time in seeking to live what they knew! To 'strive to enter the narrow door', even though we know little of the answers to our questions, would help many of us. This man had a wonderfully interesting question, *'Lord, are only a few people going to be saved?'*, but Jesus was more concerned that he should

respond to what he already knew, than that he should discover the answer to something else. So Jesus answers in an unexpected way.

2. **Jesus spoke of entering the narrow door** (13:24). It was one of His ways of speaking of fully experiencing everything that God wants to do for us. This man wanted head-knowledge, but Jesus wanted much more for him than that. He wanted the man to get through the 'narrow door' into the full blessing of the kingdom. It is not simply 'getting saved' that Jesus has in mind, or what Paul would call 'justification by faith'. 'The kingdom' means more than justification by faith, in Paul's sense of the phrase. It refers to the power of a life of godliness and ministry in the things of God.

3. **Jesus spoke of many missing the way**. There will be many people, Jesus says, who will miss the 'narrow door' of experiencing His power in their lives. To fully experience the blessings of God's kingdom we have to leave behind worldliness, the concern for worldly pleasures. We have to leave behind our pride, our love of ease, our self-protectiveness. It is difficult to squeeze through the narrow door. Some things have to be left behind.

4. **Jesus spoke of lost opportunity**. Many people will want to enter into the blessings of the godly life only when it is too late. It will be too late because the door will already be closed. Three things can 'close the door' of entry into God's kingdom-blessings: (i) the final coming of Jesus; (ii) death; (iii) the day when God 'swears in His wrath' that no further progress will be made and the door to spiritual growth is closed.

Once that door is closed – for whatever reason – many blessings of the kingdom will be lost.

5. **Jesus warned that knowing about Him will not be enough to save anyone**. In a day when the door has been closed there will be people who know 'about' Jesus, even people who met Him on the streets of Israel and who had meals with Him or heard Him preach – yet who will be excluded from the blessings of God's kingdom (13:25–27). They knew 'about' Him, but never submitted to Him.

6. **Jesus spoke of bitter regrets and deep sorrow**. There will be weeping and gnashing of teeth on that day. People who

knew a lot about Jesus will be excluded (13:28). How many will be saved? The doorway is narrow! But there will be many in the kingdom of God (13:29).

7. **Jesus spoke of surprising discoveries in the last day** (13:30). Some who were 'first' in this world will be 'last' in that day. Some who seem very insignificant in this world will be greatly rewarded with kingdom-blessings.

In the next little unit of Luke's Gospel (13:31–35) Jesus Himself gives us an example of what it means to 'strive' to do God's will.

Jesus Himself was living for God while He could. Someone warned Him that He was in danger from Herod (13:31) but Jesus was not troubled. While He was doing God's will He was in no danger (13:32–33). His death in Jerusalem would certainly be brought about by God at the right time. The thought of what would happen when people were taken by surprise in the judgement of God led Jesus into great grief. He loved Jerusalem, and would dearly have liked to gather Jerusalem to Himself (13:34) but the city was under judgement and soon would be destroyed (13:35). Roman soldiers would destroy it in AD 70. A time of weeping and gnashing of teeth was not so far away for the very people who were listening to His voice!

Strive to enter by the narrow door! Be like Jesus Himself, living for God, caring little about the dangers that come from the world's opposition. Most painful of all, we have to leave 'self' behind. This self-centredness of ours cannot be squeezed through the narrow door. *'Lord, are only a few people going to be saved?'* Jesus will not talk to us about other people; He will only say something to us about ourselves. Strive to enter by the narrow door!

# Chapter 10

## Self-centred Religion

### (Luke 14:1–14)

Jesus would often have meals with people in order to have an opportunity to talk to them. He would even spend time with people who were very critical of Him. The Pharisees were not generally friendly to Jesus, but He was happy to eat with them and talk to them.

One Saturday Jesus was eating in the home of a Pharisee. Probably Jesus had just been to the synagogue not far away; one could not walk far on a sabbath day. There was a man there suffering from 'dropsy' (14:1–2), a physical condition in which fluid builds up in the body and makes it heavy and inclined to sag. The Pharisee was not very friendly towards Jesus, and was watching Him suspiciously, wondering whether Jesus would heal someone on a Sabbath, as He had done many times before. The suffering man does not seem to be a guest. After he is healed he is sent away. Jesus does four things in response to the attitude of the Pharisees.

1. **Jesus resists their legalism**. It is difficult to find anything that Jesus ever did that was actually disobedient to any command in the law of Moses. What He deliberately disregarded was the Jewish additions to the Mosaic law. The Pharisees loved to make the Mosaic law more burdensome than it really was. It was burdensome enough in itself, but they had a tendency to make their religion a very 'heavy' matter. This is one of the difficulties of liking legislation too much. You tend to add more and more legislation to cover the gaps and make sure that no one can possibly come anywhere near disobeying the law! There are two ways of going higher than the law. One is to forget the law and walk in the Holy

Spirit. The other is to add more and more law, trying to get higher and higher in your 'obedience'. But this kind of legalism does not work. It is 'of no value in subduing the flesh' (Colossians 2:23).

People like this are very strict and rigid. They want every tiny bit of behaviour to conform to their prejudices! Jesus is not intimidated by this kind of religion. He calmly goes ahead and does what He knows will annoy them! First of all He faces the question: *'Is it lawful to heal on a Sabbath?'* (14:3). He is not afraid of them. They have no answer. Jesus goes ahead and heals the man (14:4).

2. **Jesus points out how inconsistent legalists are**. If they have an ox which is in trouble on the Sabbath they will do something about it! They do not mind 'healing' an ox of theirs which is in trouble, but they do not want Jesus to heal a man with dropsy. This goes to show how hypocritical it is to be legalistic. Such people are sometimes more legalistic about others than they are about themselves. They can have very strict religion, but somehow their rules are for other people. They 'bend the rules' when it comes to their own problems and situations. What deceitful creatures men and women are – all of us!

3. **Jesus points to the pride of religious people**. They can make no reply to His accusation of inconsistency in Sabbath-keeping. They know what He says is true. Jesus goes on to another point, concerning these Pharisees. They love honour and glory too much! When they go to a wedding they like to sit in the conspicuous places as if they are important people (14:7). Jesus says, 'Don't do it!' Let the honour come to you as a result of someone giving it to you. Don't take glory for yourself (14:8–10). People like to use religion as a way of getting attention for themselves. Jesus says seeking glory is a mark of unbelief, a mark of dead and useless religion. True faith is more concerned about honour from God, than honour from others. Of course, we all like to be honoured. Men and women were made to be 'crowned with glory and honour' (Psalm 8:5), but we lost our glory when we sinned. Only God can give it back to us, and it will only come by serving Him.

4. **While talking of feasts, Jesus points to a better way of living, one of humble generosity** (14:12–14). The proud Pharisee in his attention-seeking, proud, legalistic religion is full of his own self-importance. Better, says Jesus, to learn another way. He urges the Pharisees, and His disciples who are listening, not to have this self-centred kind of religion. When they have a public meal at their house (as the Pharisee is doing – see 14:1), they should invite the neediest people, not only those who repay the invitation. Don't be generous only with your own advantage in mind, says Jesus. It is a hint that that is what the Pharisee of 14:1 had done. He had not invited Jesus out of any love for Him! So what was his motive? He hoped to get something out of it. He had not asked the man with dropsy to stay on for lunch!

The trouble with all of us is that we are ruled by self-centredness. Sin turns us in on ourselves and we start manipulating everything for our own convenience, for our own glory and advantage. What an ugly, foul thing is this self-centredness that we call 'sin'.

Jesus is on His way to Jerusalem. He has 'set His face' to go there to die for sinners (9:51). His ministry on the way shows how much His death upon the cross is needed. Sinners like the Pharisees need to discover they have a religion with no grace in it. It is the atoning death of Jesus on the cross which humbles us, grants us forgiveness, and brings the grace of God into our lives.

# Chapter 11

# The Great Feast

(Luke 14:15–24)

Jesus liked to use opportunities for speaking about God's kingdom. Sometimes people would make random comments about some aspect of Jesus' teaching – and then Jesus would use what was said. We have already seen it in connection with Luke 12:13. Now there is another remark from the crowd (14:15) and again Jesus uses it. The man knows that the final reward of godly people will be like a great banquet and says, *'Blessed be the person who will eat at the feast . . . '* (14:15).

Jesus takes up the point and tells a parable.

1. **The kingdom of God is like a banquet with invitations which go out to many people** (14:16). The kingdom of God is like a party, a banquet! This itself deserves some meditation. The kingdom of God is not like a university – although in some places you might think so. The kingdom of God is not like a hospital – although in some places you might think so. The kingdom of God is not a mighty business empire. It is not a bank. It is not a welfare society. The kingdom of God is like a banquet! God is saying to us, 'Come! I have got everything ready for you.' There is free food – the rich food of the Word of God. There is Jesus as the bread of life! There is the Holy Spirit as the new wine of the kingdom! A banquet! The kingdom of God comes to us a gift with everything prepared (14:17). God wants us to sit down at the table of the kingdom – the thought picks up from Luke 13:28–29 as well as 14:7–13.

2. **Surprisingly, the people for whom the banquet is intended do not want it**. Jesus is referring to the people of Israel. He still has 'the leaders of the Pharisees' (14:1) in mind.

In the parable, the first people to receive an invitation to the banquet make excuses. They talk about business opportunities and their heavy responsibilities. They have just married a wife, and so cannot come (14:18–20). Jesus is still referring to the people of Israel. These are the ordinary affairs of life: business, responsibilities, getting married. These are the things that people are interested in all the time. Yet they are the kind of things that make people so preoccupied that they brush aside the infinitely greater matter, the kingdom of God.

It was a very surprising thing when the people of Israel rejected Jesus. For hundreds of years the nation of Israel had been looking for a 'Son of David' to be their Saviour. But Israel as a whole rejected Jesus. You would think that when salvation came the Jewish people would receive it. They had been promised that a Saviour would come to them. They had been praying for Messiah to come. Their scholars studied the Old Testament with great eagerness finding dozens of promises of the Messiah. Then one day the Saviour arrived! But then the very people who were the traditional people of God, wanting so much the coming of their Saviour, rejected Him when He came! *'He came to what was his own, and his own people did not receive him'* (John 1:11).

Actually history often repeats itself in this matter. Often traditional 'religious people', God's traditional people, do not like it when there is a forward move in the kingdom of God. Just as Israel was not ready for God to send His Son, so often the 'older' church is not ready when God moves in His kingdom and does something unexpected. Every spiritual revival gets some persecution from the church! People like their traditional Christianity and do not want God to do anything that disturbs it! People who were blessed in revival in one generation are traditional a few years later. They too dislike it when God does something new.

Every spiritual revival is rejected by some of God's traditional people who make excuses and criticisms and refuse to join in what God is doing. What does God do when this happens?

3. **When the first invitation is rejected, another invitation goes out to people who are entirely unsuitable!** (Luke 14:21–24). In

the parable the rich man giving the big dinner feels insulted that his original guests have declined his invitation (14:21a). So he sends out his servants to invite the most unworthy and needy people, the poor, the crippled, the blind, the lame (14:21b) – the kind of people who never get invited to banquets! (God Himself fulfils the principle of Luke 14:12–13!) Even when these guests have come, the servants still go out looking for more and more of the needy and those thought to be worthless (14:22–23). Who does Jesus have in mind? The gentiles! The rich man giving the banquet remains angry with those who turned down the invitation. God remains angry with those who got the first offer of the kingdom of God but rejected it. The religious people who were not interested in Jesus will be left out of God's final kingdom. It was true then of the many Jewish people who rejected Jesus. It is true in every generation of those who love traditional 'Christianity' but have no interest in knowing Jesus Himself and receiving the salvation that comes only through Him. Meanwhile, the gospel comes to us. We who are so unworthy. We who are needy. We are like the poor, the crippled, the blind, the lame. We have nothing with which to commend ourselves. We have been crippled in the things of God. We have been blind to God's mercy.

Yet God is still inviting us. 'Come!' He says. 'Everything is ready.' 'Come! For there is still plenty of room!' The man who first spoke to Jesus was right: *'Blessed be the person who will eat at the feast . . .'* (14:15).

# Chapter 12

## Counting the Cost
### (Luke 14:25–35)

When large crowds followed Jesus, it would lead Him to speak specially about the fact that discipleship is costly. The Sermon on the Mount was preached because of the great crowds that were listening to Jesus (see Luke 6:17). Now again as Jesus is travelling to Jerusalem, something similar happens. There are crowds of people following Him and claiming to be His disciples (14:25). Jesus gives them a word of warning. For Him, quality was as important as quantity. Jesus wanted people to come to experience His kingdom. The more disciples the better! Yet it would not be very valuable to have a great quantity of followers, if the quality of discipleship were poor. So Jesus has something to say to them about the sacrifice and dedication that is required if His disciples are to inherit what God wants to give them.

1. **We must put discipleship above closeness to friends and family**. We have to 'hate' even people who are close to us if they get in the way of our responding to Jesus and His call upon our lives. 'Hate' is a relative term. It means to love God's will so much that in comparison what we feel for others is like hate. It means that we vastly prefer the will of God, above our love for those dearest and nearest to us.

When we seek to reap the blessings of God's kingdom, we may get some surprises. Sometimes our closest relatives and friends will be opposed to our having any kind of zeal for God and His kingdom. At such a point we have to put God above those who are most precious to us.

2. **We must put discipleship above our love of ourselves**. Jesus says, *'If anyone comes to me and does not hate ... even his own*

44

*life – he cannot be my disciple'* (14:26). We love ourselves a lot! We love our reputation, our comfort, our pleasures, our security. But if we are to reap the blessings of the kingdom of God, we must deliberately put these in second place.

Jesus did not want anyone to follow Him carelessly or lightly. He gave advance warning that we have to lose our lives in order to find them.

3. **We must accept the painful 'crucifixions' God sends to us**. If we are to make progress in our experience of God, and in being used by Him, we shall need preparation. One kind of preparation God sends upon us consists of 'crucifixions', experiences that are very painful, but if we accept them they will bring immense blessing in our lives (14:27). What are these 'crucifixions'? It may be suffering that we have to go through without bitterness or complaining. It may be delay or opposition. It may be enmity from others that we have to handle without resentment. Or the thing that 'crucifies' us may be giving up something that is not God's will for our lives. It may be swallowing our pride. But God is likely to send something to us that is extremely painful. It was the habit of Roman soldiers to force a man about to be crucified to carry his own cross. He had to assist in his own crucifixion. God asks us to do something similar in our spiritual experience.

4. **Jesus asks us to consider this costliness of the kingdom**. He puts it to the disciples – and to us as well – in terms of two illustrations (14:28–30, 31–33). We are being asked to face this matter ahead of time. It will not be much use when some crisis comes to start deciding whether we want God's kingdom. Jesus asks us to consider the matter now, before the crisis comes.

If a man is about to build a tower will he not, before he starts building, consider what it is going to cost (14:28–30)?

5. **Jesus asks us to consider the power of the enemy, and the fierceness of the battle** (14:31–33). If an army general is about to start a battle, will he not consider, before he starts fighting, whether he is willing to endure everything that will be needed for him to get victory (14:31–33)?

6. **What is needed is 'saltiness' – distinctiveness and sharp purity**. Jesus says, *'Salt is good, but if it loses its saltiness, how*

*can it be made salty again?'* (14:34). Salt was famous for its sharp taste. It used to be rubbed into meat to keep the meat from going bad. The Christian needs to be 'salty', sharply different from the world. If, as life goes forward, we lose this 'sharpness of taste', it ruins our usefulness to God.

Once this 'saltiness' has been lost, it is not easy to recover. If we compromise with sin we may be forgiven, but our usefulness to God might be lost beyond recovery. If we eventually become spiritually deaf, there is no recovery.

7. **What will be needed is attentiveness to what God says to us**. We stay 'salty' by continually hearing from God (14:35). *'He that has ears to hear, let that person hear,'* says Jesus. Some are so spiritually deaf that they don't even have ears. Others have been woken up by God, and they are able to hear. They have ears to hear – but even then some don't hear. The world does not have ears for Jesus. Disciples have ears, but not all of them hear. So Jesus says, *'He that has ears to hear, let that person hear.'* We need two things, not one. First, we need ears: we need the Holy Spirit to make us new people so that we are able to hear God. But then there is a second thing: now that we have ears, we need to actually hear. Hearing and responding is the way forward in the kingdom of God.

# Chapter 13

## A Lost Sheep and a Lost Coin
### (Luke 15:1–10)

Jesus was popular with tax collectors (corrupt and oppressive people working for the Roman government) and with sinners (people who were not welcomed in the synagogues). He was so gracious to them. They did not feel humiliated by Him. Although He often spoke of the need for repentance, sinners also felt that He loved them. They drew near to listen to Him very willingly (15:1).

But the Pharisees did not like it (15:2)! Many religious people lose sight of God's grace. They begin by wanting people to be holy (that's fine!), but they often forget that it is the **grace** of God that *'trains us ... to live sober, upright and godly lives'* (Titus 2:12). The Bible tells us to grow in **grace** (2 Peter 3:18). Religious people generally think we need numerous regulations in order to be godly. They have their version of the law of God – generally the Ten Commandments with various alterations and additions – and then they add to it (because the law does not seem to work they add more law to the law). The result is bondage and hypocrisy. The Pharisees were the greatest example of this kind of 'heavy' religion in Jesus' day. They did not like the grace of God, and they were critical of Jesus when He was sweet and pleasant to sinful people.

So Jesus tries to help the Pharisees by telling them three parables: one about a lost sheep, one about a lost loin, and one about a lost son.

1. **Jesus loved to go after the worst kind of person – and so should we**. He put the matter in terms of a story. Imagine, says Jesus, a shepherd with a hundred sheep to look after. Sheep

are such foolish creatures. They wander away and get lost. They get tangled up in thorns and bushes. They fall down pits and cracks in the ground. When that happens, the shepherd leaves most of his sheep to look after themselves, while he goes looking for the one that is in trouble (15:3–4).

When Jesus ministered in this world, He concentrated specially on the worst sinners. Tax collectors and sinners excluded from the synagogue were of special interest to Him. He loved to go after people who really needed a Saviour. This is what the grace of God is like.

2. **Jesus was persistent in seeking those who were in bad trouble**. The good shepherd looks for the lost sheep, and he persists in looking 'until he finds it' (15:4). The grace of God does not abandon us or easily give up on us. The shepherd persists in his search hour after hour until he finds the wanderer.

3. **Jesus is like the shepherd in carrying those who need carrying**. The shepherd, when he has at last found the lost sheep, *'joyfully lays it on his shoulders'* (15:5). When at last he finds the lost sheep, it perhaps is worn and hungry and weak. The shepherd carries it back home. Jesus often carries us. He likes to **lead** His people, but when they are at their worst He has to **carry** them, and like a good shepherd that is what He does.

4. **Jesus is like the shepherd in calling for celebration when one wanderer is found**. The shepherd who finds his lost sheep *'calls together his friends and his neighbours, saying to them, "Rejoice with me…"'* (15:6). The shepherd gets joy over rescuing his wanderer. For the moment he is more delighted with the one than he is with the ninety-nine. It is the same even in heaven, says Jesus (15:7). Heaven is a place of grace. The Pharisees may not be rejoicing over Jesus' eating with wicked people, but the angels are enjoying it! There is much graciousness among the angels.

To the parable of the lost sheep, Jesus adds the parable of the lost coin (15:8–10). **It makes the same point, but specially emphasises the persistence with which Jesus seeks the sinner**. A silver coin was very valuable to the ordinary people of ancient Israel, and in the dark houses in which they lived a lost coin might be difficult to find. The woman of the house might search for hours looking for her lost treasure.

Tax collectors and sinners were often to be found with Jesus. He would spend a lot of time with them and would often eat with them. This is because He was making great efforts to win them for the kingdom of God. He was being like the woman who sweeps right through the house looking in every possible corner to find where the coin might have dropped.

Jesus is explaining His ministry to the Pharisees and to any in the crowd who might be affected by what the Pharisees are saying about Jesus. The Pharisees' religion is about law. Jesus' message is about God's graciousness. The Pharisees kept sinners out of the synagogues. Jesus drew them to Himself. The Pharisees were intimidating and threatening to sinners. Jesus was warm and reassuring and inviting.

People who are gripped by God's grace will themselves be gracious. The Pharisees were stern and critical of sinners. They grumbled when Jesus showed loving graciousness towards disreputable characters. That is because they themselves had not come to a realisation of God's grace in their own lives. When we see that we too can relate to God only because of His kindness and graciousness towards us, then we are delighted that God is gracious to us, and happy for Him to be gracious to everyone else. Hostility towards sinners is a sign that we think we don't need Jesus' salvation. Those who are gripped by an awareness of God's grace will always want more people to be added to His kingdom.

# Chapter 14

## A Lost Son
### (Luke 15:11–21)

God wants us to see 'the riches of His grace' (see Ephesians 1:7). The Pharisees were angry and critical of Jesus because He was so friendly to sinners. In response to their anger at His graciousness, He told the people three parables. The third one – the parable of the lost son – really focuses on three characters. There is the lost son, the waiting father, and the elder brother. We learn something from all three. Consider first the son who ruined his life.

1. **Sin often begins with self-confidence**. The young man was quite confident that he would be able to run his own life without the help of his father. He wanted money (15:11–12) and independence (15:13), and he wanted to put a distance between himself and his father (in a 'far country'). He was quite sure that he would enjoy life if he was given this kind of freedom.

In Israel, it was possible for a father to share out some of the property that would eventually come to his son. In Israel – unlike some other cultures – this did not have to wait until the father died. So the younger son is impatient for the money that would one day come to him. He wants it **now**. He is self-confident and impatient.

2. **Sin is deceitful**. When the young man broke free from his father and began living his own wicked life, he did not realise how easily sin deceives us. He thought his independence from his father would lead to happiness and pleasure, but his foolishness brought him into troubles he had never expected. Sin offers us pleasure, but it is not long before it ruins our lives. Soon the young man began to find himself in need.

3. **Sin leads us into helplessness in a time of emergency**. Famine came to the land where the prodigal had gone to seek his pleasures. Life was all right for him as long as his money was lasting, but then something unexpected happened: a famine (15:14). Soon he was in a terrible crisis, and ended up feeding pigs and even wanting to eat the pigs' food (15:15–16). Living away from his father had seemed a good idea at the time, but soon what the son did brought him pain and distress.

4. **Recovery began when the lost son admitted his need**. Two things had to happen for the lost son to recover. First, he had to 'come to himself' (15:17–19). He was in such a terrible situation and it had all started from the day when he had left his father. There is a spiritual equivalent. God wishes to be our Father and asks us to come back to Him. But recovery will start when we 'come to ourselves', when we see the predicament we are in, alienated from our heavenly Father.

There was a second stage. He had to turn around and start going back home (15:20). The father was waiting, but the son had to turn around if he was ever to get back to his father. If we are to be reconciled to God, we have to 'come to ourselves', and then turn round and start moving back to God, away from the life of wickedness.

The second character in the parable is the waiting father. In the parable, the father obviously stands for God.

1. **God is eager for sinners to return to Him**. The father of the parable was more eager to have the son back than the son ever realised. Every day the father was looking out for his son's return. On the very day the son was making his way back, the father was looking for him and saw him coming long before he was near to the house (15:20b).

2. **God responds with love when we turn to Him**. The father ran to greet his son. It is an extraordinary picture. Fathers in ancient Israel would not generally have done anything as undignified as running, but the father of the parable runs in delight to greet his returning son! He is full of love. He embraces him and kisses him.

3. **God insists on receiving us back on the basis of grace alone**. In the far country the son had prepared a little speech to say

to his father: *'I have sinned ... I am no longer worthy to be called your son. Make me like one of your hired workers'* (15:19). The son believed his father would welcome him back but thought he would have to come back as a slave. He thought his sonship had been sinned away, and the best he could hope for was that his father would accept him as a hired worker.

So the son starts his little prepared speech: *'I have sinned ... I am no longer worthy to be called your son...'*. But he never gets to saying 'Make me like one of your hired workers'. Before he can even finish his speech the father interrupts him! He welcomes him, calls for robe to given to him, a ring to be put on his son's finger, sandals on his feet. The son is not to try to 'earn' his way back to the father. The father takes him as he is. He will come back as a son not as a slave!

A parable does not try to teach everything in one attempt. We must not press this parable because of things it does not mention (the cross, the work of the Spirit). It makes only a few limited and simple points. One of them is the amazing graciousness of God in receiving back those who have wandered far from Him. It must be remembered that the parable relates to the situation in Luke 15:1–2. Jesus welcomes the worst sinner to come to get to know Him.

# *Chapter 15*

## The Angry Brother
(Luke 15:22–32)

The third figure in the parable of the lost son is the elder brother. He stands for the Pharisees, who had been so critical of Jesus and His friends. The older brother comes along and hears music and dancing (15:25). He finds out that his younger brother has come home, and has been given a warm welcome (15:26–27), but his only response to his father's generosity is one of anger and withdrawal (15:28a). His father is still gracious even to his angry older son. He has to come out (15:28b) to explain how he views what is happening. The older brother is as much a son of the father as the younger son, but the father specially rejoices in the recovery of his more obviously rebellious son (15:29–32).

**It is possible to claim loyalty to God and yet be very ignorant of His grace**. The Pharisees thought of themselves as 'good' people. They were outwardly moral. They attended the synagogues for worship every Sabbath. They claimed to be law-abiding people. They disliked 'tax collectors' (who were employed by the Romans and were greedy for money) and 'sinners' (people who did not keep the Pharisees' regulations). They wanted to be loyal to God, yet they had lost sight of God's grace. These were the people who grumbled at Jesus because He ate with tax collectors and sinners (see 15:1–2).

The older son represents good religious people who somehow think that because they are externally law-abiding they are acceptable to God. But the older son, and the religious people he represents, have some characteristics they have not thought about.

1. **'Good' people think that they are accepted by God because of how good they are**. The older brother thinks he is a good son to his father. He has not sinned in the disgraceful way that his younger brother has. This is precisely how a certain kind of religious person thinks. He is a good son to God, he thinks, because he has behaved so well in public and has not disgraced himself.

2. **Such a 'good' person hates the grace of God**. He thinks the grace of God is too easy, too cheap, and is scornful of what he considers is an 'easy' salvation. 'This fellow welcomes sinners and eats with them!' the Pharisees said with scorn. 'This son of yours!' says the elder brother scornfully.

3. **'Older brothers' are sinners too, but their sins are more subtle**. The older son was angered by his father's generosity and kindness. He did not like it that his father was so compassionate towards his wayward son. He thought that he himself was fully obedient to his father. He feels worthy of special treatment by his father. Yet all of this is wickedly sinful – just as the younger son's wild living was wickedly sinful. The older brother's spirit is entirely wrong. He is sarcastic about his younger brother. He omits any respectful way of speaking to his father. He feels that he has been a slave for his father (the very thing that the father did not want!).

The older brother's sins are self-righteousness ('never did I disobey your command'), resentment ('you never gave me a goat') and bitterness ('this son of yours!'), which show themselves in his anger and self-exclusion.

4. **The hero of the story is the father**. He treats both sons well. He waits patiently and lovingly for the younger son to return, but he also responds patiently and lovingly to the elder brother. The elder brother stays away from the father, but the father does not stay away from him. The elder brother takes no initiative in seeking friendship with either his father or his younger brother, but the father takes the initiative in seeking reconciliation with his older son, and also tries to get the older son to be pleasant to his younger brother. The elder brother speaks of 'this son of yours'; the father speaks of 'this your brother', gently correcting the older son's attitude.

There is no mention of any atonement for sin in the parable

of the lost son, but we should not make any special deductions from this. Parables are not intended to teach a wide range of doctrine. They have one or two main points, at most three. One should not expect them to have teaching other than the few central points that each parable makes. It is important to remember that this parable is being given as Jesus is steadily making His way to Jerusalem to die. Luke has already told us that Jesus has 'set His face' to go to Jerusalem (9:51). The parable of the lost son is not isolated; it comes in a setting where Jesus is travelling to Jerusalem to die as a sacrifice for sins. God is a 'waiting Father' because the sacrifice for sins is about to be made. As for ourselves, we may know that God is reconciled to us in the cross of Jesus; now God 'waits' for us to be reconciled to Him. 'Younger sons' (wild and rebellious people who have ruined their lives) and 'older brothers' (respectable people who are thought to be law-abiding) are both in need of the graciousness of their Father. The Father waits for the prodigal to come back; and He waits for the law-abiding people to come inside. The surprising thing is that prodigals often come home from a far country but the law-abiding people do not come inside the place where everyone is celebrating. The elder son is not in a far country; he is nearby, but he still stands outside and misses the party. The one from a far country discovers grace. The older brother in the next room misses it.

# Chapter 16

## The Day of Settling Accounts
### (Luke 16:1–18)

A rich man has a 'steward' – a financial manager – but one day he hears that his financial manager has been neglecting his duties; money has been lost. So the owner of the business asks for a full account of what has been happening to the money. The manager knows that he is about to lose his job (16:2–3) and is worried about his future.

So he comes to a decision that will give him some help in the future when he no longer has his work of being the steward of the rich man's property (16:4). He uses his last remaining days to find a way of protecting himself. He calls each of the owner's debtors (16:5). One of them owes money for a hundred measures of oil, worth about 1000 denarii (three years' wages for a labouring man). He is allowed to write a fresh document for half the amount (16:6). He calls another debtor. This one owes money for a hundred measures of wheat, worth about 2500 denarii. It too is drastically reduced (16:7). 'The master' in verse 8a probably refers to the rich man (since it is the same word as that used in 16:3). The owner of the business is forced to admit that the 'manager' has prepared skilfully for the future. He has used the short time left in his stewardship to benefit others, so that later others would be grateful to him.

What the steward did was quite legal. He had a certain amount of freedom in his work and, in the short time left, he used this freedom for his own advantage. Worldly people use their possessions to their own advantage. Why should spiritual people not use theirs for their **eternal** advantage?

56

What are the lessons of the parable?

**God's day of reckoning will deal with the way we have used our possessions**.

1. God is the owner of everything we have; we're only stewards and managers.

2. There is only a short time left for us in our stewardship. Soon the Owner is to come and our time in this world, managing what God gives us, will come to an end.

3. If we are wise we will use our resources now with our eye on what will happen to us on the day of judgement. We will use all that God has given us with a view to what He will require of us on the day of judgement. This is the main point of the parable: *'Make friends for yourselves by means of worldly wealth, so that when it fails they may receive you into the eternal dwellings'* (16:9). It means: use your money with an eye on your eternal future. Use it in such a way that it supports God's kingdom and there are people in heaven because you have supported God's work. In the next parable (16:19–30), the rich man did not use any of his wealth to help Lazarus. Lazarus died first, before the rich man, but the rich man was not welcomed into heaven by Lazarus! Use your money in such a way that in the afterlife there are people who are grateful to God because of you.

Luke 16:10–13 follows up the parable. The way you use a little wealth shows what you are really like. If God can trust you with little, you will be given more and so you will be able to demonstrate your faithfulness in the use of more. If you are not faithful in what belongs to God (the money you manage for Him), will He give you what is your own (heavenly reward for your faithfulness)? If you are financially unfaithful, you cannot be serving God. No one can serve two masters at the same time. If you live for God, you will not live for money. If you live for money, you will not live for God.

Luke 16:14–15 is another comment continuing the theme of faithfulness in the use of money. The Pharisees were so religious and pretended to be superior to others, but they were greedy for money. Their wealth was admired and envied by many but God knew the state of their hearts. Where there is no financial honesty, there is no approval from God.

God's day of reckoning will deal with other things besides the use of money.

**God's day of reckoning will deal with openness to God**. The Pharisees loved the law of Moses. They were not open to there ever coming a day when it would end. But the law and prophets were pointing to Jesus (16:16). Once Jesus has come it is time to realise that a new day has arrived. It is time for aggressive faith [1] in Jesus. But the Pharisees preferred to hold on to the old covenant of Moses. They loved the Mosaic law but were no longer open to God. The law cannot be pushed aside; it has to be fulfilled (16:17). The Pharisees needed to see that Jesus was its fulfilment. But some people refused to believe it was a day of fulfilment, a day when God was doing new things.

**God's day of reckoning will deal with unfaithfulness in marriage**. Generally speaking – there may be exceptions – ending a marriage will bring down the anger of God (16:18).

Luke's next parable will take up in fuller detail the form that the anger of God will take in His day of reckoning. It will speak of torment (16:23) and anguish (16:24). And it will speak of one who was carried by angels to God's heaven. God's day of reckoning will have consequences that last forever.

## Note

1. See, more fully, my exposition in *How To Enjoy God's Worldwide Church* (1995, re-issued by Paternoster), pp. 23–25.

# Chapter 17

## The Rich Man and Lazarus
### (Luke 16:19–31)

The parable of the rich man and Lazarus is unusual. The characters do not symbolise people different from themselves (as, for example, in another parable the sower represents Jesus). They represent people in **similar** situations: Lazarus represents the poor; the rich man represents all rich people who are careless and self-centred; Abraham does not stand for anyone other than himself. So this is not the kind of parable in which the characters and situations symbolise something totally **different** from those in the story (as elsewhere the soils might symbolise disciples, and treasure might symbolise God's kingdom, and an estate-manager's day of accounting might represent God's judgement day). This makes me think that the description of Hades is to be taken fairly seriously. It must not be pressed too much. For example, I do not think the parable teaches that people in Hades talk to Abraham, or that people in heaven might want to visit Hades, or that people in Hades are concerned about their brothers. These details are surely only part of the picture language. But there are other aspects which probably are to be taken more seriously. The parable deals with the time immediately after death. It is mainly a parable about the use of riches, and teaches three main lessons about wealth.

1. **Wealth cannot be taken beyond the grave**. At the moment of death wealth has to be left behind. The story reminds us that people's lifestyles can vary so much. The rich man was dressed in expensive clothes (purple material was expensive), and in comfortable garments (fine linen). He ate well and was enjoying his affluent life (16:19). Not far away, however, was a

person living a very different lifestyle. Lazarus was homeless, sick, hungry and without any protection from troublesome dogs (16:20–21). It seems to be taken for granted that Lazarus is a godly man, and that the rich man is not. The assumption is a reasonable one. God has chosen the poor (James 2:5); the wealthy find their riches block their way to experiencing the kingdom of God. Only because *'with God all things are possible'* (Mark 10:27) can a wealthy person experience God's kingdom.

There is nothing good about poverty, nothing bad about wealth. Abraham was rich! It all depends what you do with your wealth or your poverty. The rich man had Lazarus at his gate – but did nothing for him. But wealth only lasts for this life and death is a time of great reversal. The godly but poor man was taken by the angels to heaven ('Abraham's bosom' is a way of speaking of heaven). But the careless, heartless, rich man went to Hades (16:22–23) – the place of the dead. There his punishment for his sins began immediately, and his riches could not help him.

2. **Wealth brings God's wrath upon us if it is not used compassionately.** The rich man went to an early stage of punishment, experiencing the anger of God in 'Hades'. This word can be used (i) of the realm of the dead without defining whether bliss or punishment is involved (as in Acts 2:2), and (ii), as here, of a place of punishment. The rich man is being punished immediately after death. He does not have to wait for the day of resurrection. The Greek word *Gehenna* (the more common word for 'hell' but not used in Luke 16) is used of punishment after the resurrection. Judgement is determined by this life, decided at death, experienced from death onwards, publicised and confirmed in the final resurrection.

The rich man is not being punished because he is rich. He is experiencing God's fiery anger because he was heartless and lacking in compassion.

Judgement takes place immediately after death. Both the saved and the lost are conscious after death. The saved are happy; the lost are in agonising pain. Failure to use one's wealth for God will bring judgement in the life to come.

Hell is the absence of mercy. The rich man who had given no mercy to Lazarus now begged for mercy, but found none. *'Blessed are the merciful, for they shall receive mercy,'* says Jesus (Matthew 5:7). The rich man showed no mercy and received no mercy (16:24).

Hell is a place of jealousy. The rich man could see and envy Lazarus. There is no repentance in Hades. The rich man, who as a Jew regarded himself as a child of Abraham, still presumed his requests to Abraham would be bound to be answered. He thought the class-system of earth still applied beyond the grave and wanted to use Lazarus as a servant! Sheer pain does not in itself makes anyone repent. Hell does not bring spiritual insight. The rich man knew Lazarus by name but had done nothing to help him.

Hell is a place of pain. The rich man was in agony. Hell is a place of compensation and repayment. Both of the men who have died are being repaid. Lazarus is receiving the rewards of his patience. The rich man is receiving the retribution for his heartlessness (16:25).

Hell is the end of opportunity. The poor man cannot come to the rescue of the rich man in Hades. The rich man cannot escape (16:26).

3. **The lesson about how we use our wealth must be taken from the Word of God; nothing saves us from Hades except paying attention to what the written Word of God says about Jesus** (16:27–30). The rich man thought a miraculous visit from someone from hell to his brothers would lead them to salvation. Not so. The only way of salvation is to put faith in what God's written Word says. If the brothers will not listen to the written Word of God – Moses and the prophets – nothing else will lead them to true faith in Jesus.

# Chapter 18

## Lessons for Disciples
### (Luke 17:1–10)

Jesus is still travelling towards Jerusalem. Along the way He gives instruction to the crowd and to the disciples. Luke 17:1–10 contains four challenges to the disciples.

1. **A disciple must avoid putting stumbling blocks in front of others** (17:1–3a). 'Stumbling blocks must come' or (more literally translated) 'It is impossible for stumbling blocks not to come'.

A 'stumbling block' is a cause of sin. It is not simply something that causes surprise. Sometimes a Christian might say to another Christian, 'You have made me stumble' – when all that he means is that he is surprised at what the other person did. In some parts of the world over-conservative people like to claim that they have been 'made to stumble'. But being 'made to stumble' is being led into **sin**. We must not criticise other Christians, just because they are different from ourselves. Causing someone to stumble is to cause someone to sin.

Jesus' concern is that we ourselves should not become a 'stumbling block' to another disciple. God gets angry if we lead another person into sin. Better to be drowned and end our life prematurely than face the anger of God in which some of our reward in heaven is lost because our lives have had an impact for the worse. *'Take heed to yourselves,'* says Jesus (17:3a).

2. **A disciple must practise unlimited forgiveness** (17:3b–4). These verses are linked with the previous ones. We seek to help each other not to sin, but when someone in the fellowship does sin, what then? Jesus says: *'If your brother sins, rebuke*

*him'* (17:3b). Disciples have a responsibility to admonish each other. Of course, we have to be sure it really is sin that we are dealing with. But if we see a brother or sister in the Lord clearly sinning, we are urged to go to him and as lovingly as possible rebuke him. It takes great humility and loving skill! What we tend to do is get bitter about another person's sin or complain to our friends or visit the pastor with our complaint. Jesus says: go and see the person concerned!

Then: *'if he repents, forgive him'* (17:3c). We are forbidden to continue in hostility. We are forbidden to hold a grudge.

We might ask: what if the person does not repent? Matthew 18:16–17 tells us more. But there still has to be a forgiving **attitude** in us, even when it might not be possible to assure the other person that he or she is forgiven – because he or she shows no signs of repentance. But even towards 'a Gentile or a tax collector' (Matthew 18:17) our attitude still has to be one of forgiveness.

If a brother or sister has a problem with one particular sin, the forgiving might have to go on for a long time (17:4).

3. **A disciple must seek increase of faith** (17:5–6). The disciples ask that their faith might be increased (17:5). What exactly, I wonder, did they expect Jesus to do? Were they wanting a miraculous increase of faith to take place in their hearts by the decree of Jesus?

Jesus does not seem to say much about how to increase faith. He simply describes the very great value and power of faith (17:6). It is not **quantity** of faith that concerns Him. What matters is whether faith is real. Even small faith will perform mighty works if it is real and would give the disciple great confidence (17:6).

What then is 'faith'? It is not some inward virtue in us. It is not something that we have to 'work up'. It is not trying to persuade ourselves of something, or pretending that we be certain of something.

Faith is believing God. It is trusting God's word to us in Scripture. It is trusting God's word to us through the Holy Spirit. It is trusting in God's character, His mercy, His power. But faith is not faith in itself. It is not faith in faith. The great thing about faith is that it looks to God. Faith is seeing God's greatness, hearing His voice, knowing His truthfulness and reliability.

Jesus does not seem to say much about increasing faith. His way of answering the disciples' request is simply to describe to them the great power of faith. Then they will want to believe more and more of the promises of God. And their faith will grow, as God honours the faith that they have.

4. **Disciples must regard themselves as duty-bound to serve God** (17:7–10). The disciples must be careful not to get so proud of themselves that they start thinking they are superior creatures, and that God owes them something. We are God's slaves; God is not our slave! Slaves do not usually get invited to dine with the master. Rather the master relaxes while the slaves do the work! When they have finished, they do not get very much praise or special gratitude. They are expected to work! The slave must say, *'We are unworthy slaves; we have only done what we ought to have done'* (17:10). Disciples are the same. We are duty-bound to serve God and His kingdom. We were rescued from the ugly bondage of sin and have become the willing happy slaves of the Lord Jesus Christ. But we must not start getting proud of ourselves and think that God is duty-bound towards us. We are not 'entitled' to special favour from God. At best we are people who are being shown mercy. We can be confident in God's love. We can be sure of our acceptance with God. But still at our best we have no right to complain, no right to demand an easy life. We are duty-bound to serve God in any way He requests. Our greatest blessings come when we stay as His 'unworthy servants'.

# Chapter 19

## Gratitude and Salvation

### (Luke 17:11–21)

There is perhaps a connection between Luke 17:11–21 and the preceding three verses, because the Gospel of Luke goes on to speak about some people who did not regard themselves as duty-bound to serve God.

Jesus is still on His last journey towards Jerusalem (17:11). There was a road that ran along the border between Galilee and Samaria. Somewhere along the way Jesus entered a Samaritan village and healed ten lepers (17:12), who must all have been Samaritans.

1. **It is possible to have a self-centred belief in the supernatural without having saving faith in Jesus.** Are these lepers believers in Jesus Christ? Will we meet them in heaven? They had a belief in the supernatural; and they believed that Jesus could heal them. They depended on Jesus to show special mercy to them (17:13). Jesus told them to follow the legal requirement of the Mosaic law which said that any person who thought he was healed had to have it certified by a priest (17:14). The ten men were sufficiently confident in Jesus' ability to heal them that they did as they were told and were healed.

But there are plenty of people who believe in the supernatural without having faith in Jesus the Saviour. These ten men thought that Jesus would be able to heal them, and they were right. Jesus could and did heal them. Yet they failed to enter fully into the salvation that Jesus was bringing. Nine of them were the opposite of what Jesus had asked for in 17:7–10. They are so self-centred that they feel God owes them something. They have no special gratitude, but are simply (no doubt) pleased to have been so fortunate as to be healed! Once they have got what they want from Jesus they have no further interest in Him.

People often come to Jesus for earthly blessings without wanting to serve God or change their lives in a way that will please Him. Belief in miracles ought to lead on to a higher kind of faith, or (it would be better to say) faith in Jesus as the Saviour and as the One who wants to use us in a life of gratitude and obedience.

2. **Jesus only speaks of one of these ten men coming to salvation** (17:19). One of the ten men knows that he is not 'entitled' to special favour from God. He was a Samaritan, and the Samaritans had always opposed the idea that God would send salvation through something that would happen in Jerusalem.

Trouble tends to drive us to God but it does not always drive us to salvation. Nine of these men were driven to Jesus because they were in trouble. There is nothing wrong with that. God uses the troubles of life to bring us to Himself. Needy people listen to the gospel more eagerly than people living an easy kind of life. In the time of Jesus it was very difficult for anyone with any kind of 'leprosy'. It was not the same as the modern disease. Even a poor skin condition could be called 'leprosy'. Such people were rejected by society. Their life was cut off from other people. Such people were rejected by society. Their life was cut off from other people. The reason why the lepers cried 'from a distance' (17:12) was because they were not allowed to come near to other people. So the situation of the leper was a very miserable and desperate one. *'He shall dwell alone,'* said Leviticus 13:46.

People in desperate trouble are willing to turn to God. And God often hears the cries and pleas even of people who are not reconciled to Him and have not yet received His Son as the Saviour of the world. When God hears our desperate pleas and cries to Him, it is His way of encouraging us to submit to Him. Yet there are many who want what God has to give but then they forget God altogether.

3. **One way in which faith shows itself is to respond with gratitude to Jesus**. One man of the ten returned to express his

gratitude to Jesus. This was the sign that God had worked in his heart as well as in his body.

He was a man who knew he was unworthy. He was a Samaritan! The people of Samaria were the traditional enemies of the people of Israel. This man knew that there was no reason why Jesus should specially have healed him. He knew himself to be unworthy.

Yet he also believed Jesus would accept him despite his unworthiness as a Samaritan. He believed in the mercy of Jesus for him personally. He wanted a continuing contact with Jesus, in addition to the healing of his body. This was what made him different from the others. The others want a blessing from God but they do not specially want continuing contact with Jesus. This man has faith in Jesus' goodness and wants to return to have further dealings with Him.

Jesus says, *'Your faith has saved you.'* He must be referring to more than the healing of the body. They had all been healed but this man had something the other nine did not have: salvation in the fullest sense of the word.

Everyone knew that Jesus was going to Jerusalem. He was making it very clear. Samaritans did not like Jerusalem but this Samaritan had faith in a Saviour who was on His way to die in Jerusalem. How much he knew of the message of salvation we cannot say, but he was receiving a Saviour who was on His way to die for the sins of the world.

It is wonderful to have Jesus answer our prayers. It is more wonderful when we show our gratitude to Him and want a continuing relationship with Him.

# Chapter 20

## The Coming of the Kingdom
### (Luke 17:20–37)

As Jesus continues on His last journey to Jerusalem, the Pharisees raise a question about the kingdom of God.

1. **There is a worldly way of seeking the kingdom of God**. The Pharisees' approach to the kingdom of God was very nationalistic. They thought the 'kingdom of God' consisted largely of political influence and the release of Israel from colonial oppression by the Romans. The kingdom would come – so they thought – when God sent a mighty military hero to release them from domination by Rome. There are still people who take 'the kingdom' in a very political and earthly manner.

The Pharisees were also interested in 'signs' of the coming kingdom. When Jesus' disciples asked, *'When ... And what will be the sign ...?'* (21:7), they were asking the two questions that the Pharisees asked. People would point to events that were happening in their own day and say 'Here it is!' or 'There it is!', interpreting the events as 'signs'. The same mentality is common today. It is an approach to prophecy that is interested in intellectual puzzles more than in experiencing God.

2. **The kingdom of God is available now!** The sign-seeking approach is entirely wrong. Jesus said, *'It is not by observation that the kingdom of God comes, nor will they say, "Look, it is here! There it is!" ...'* (17:20). When worldly people like the Pharisees try to guess when the kingdom of God will come with power, they are missing the kingdom of God in their lives altogether.

Jesus says: *'...because, in fact, the kingdom of God is among you.'* The kingdom of God is God's acting in power through

68

his Son who is the King! If the King is present, the kingdom of God is present. The question is not: when will the kingdom of God come? It is here already. The question is: when will you enter the kingdom of God? God wants to act in power in your life, through Jesus. He wants Jesus to be your King. The kingdom has come! It is Jesus' acting as King. It is Jesus' producing righteousness in our lives.

3. **The kingdom of God comes in stages**. It has come; it is coming; it will come. Right now the kingdom of God is coming in the lives of all who submit to Jesus. Yet the **present** coming of the kingdom is not irresistible or over-powering. It is possible to miss what is happening. One day the kingdom of God will appear in glorious power. One stage of the kingdom is present already, but it will end dramatically when another stage of the kingdom comes, in overwhelming power and irresistible glory.

4. **The secret to enjoying the future coming of the kingdom is to receive it now**. The Pharisees were wanting the kingdom of God to come, but they assumed that it would involve the exaltation of Israel, and that they would be involved in these blessings. Jesus says: the kingdom of God is here now! Be part of the future blessings of the kingdom by receiving the power of God into your life now!

'The time will come when you will long to see one of the days of the Son of Man, but you will not see it' (17:22). Jesus is referring to the period that is just about to come. He is walking towards Jerusalem. He knows that times of great trouble are ahead. The disciples will long for God's kingdom to come to Israel, but there will be days of great difficulty. 'The days of the Son of Man' refers to days when the royal power of God is strong. The disciples will want days of evangelistic success for Israel, but it will be delayed and Israel will go through times of suffering.

At such a time they must not be misled by prophetic cranks trying to guess what is happening from the 'signs of the times' (17:23). When Jesus comes there will be no need for guess-work! A flash of lightning is sudden and startling and is seen by everyone. Jesus' 'coming' – both finally and (by way of anticipation) repeatedly during the course of history – will be dramatic (17:24). If people want to know what must come before it, the answer is: the suffering of Jesus on the cross (17:25)!

We may want the kingdom of God to come dramatically and long for the 'days of the Son of Man' – the Spirit of God working in great power – to be present. But for much of the time the kingdom of God comes quietly, through childlike faith (see 18:17). I must experience the kingdom of God **now** by childlike faith.

5. **When future manifestations of the kingdom come, they will come suddenly**. Luke 17:26–36 is not referring only to the final 'Second Coming' of Jesus, but to the **many** times and ways in which sudden judgement comes. He especially has in mind the fall of Jerusalem, which took place in AD 70. This is clear because of verses 31–36. No one will worry about going back home to collect possessions in the final 'coming' of Jesus. (The similar verses in Mark 13:15–18 clearly refer to the fall of Jerusalem; and the whole of Luke 21:5–33 refers to the fall of Jerusalem as 21:32 makes clear.)

When do these sudden judgements come? Verse 37 gives the answer: vultures gather where there is a corpse. When God sees the time is ripe, the Son of man comes in judgement. In AD 70, after Israel had been given much opportunity to receive Jesus, the vultures would gather. That is, the Roman armies would come. The Pharisees got excited about exciting and interesting matters of prophecy. They would do better to receive the kingdom of God into their lives **now** and be ready for sudden judgements at any time.

# Chapter 21

## The Unjust Judge

(Luke 18:1–8)

One of the major themes of Luke's Gospel is prayer. The gospel opens with the prayers of Zacharias (1:8, 13, 67–80) and the praises of Mary (1:46–55) and the angels (2:10–20, 25–38). It portrays Jesus at prayer at His baptism (3:22), and often after that time (5:16; 6:12–13, 28). He was praying at the time of the transfiguration (9:28–29).

Also, there is much teaching in Luke's Gospel about prayer. We have had the parable of the friend at midnight (11:1–13). In the opening story of the gospel especially we learnt the danger of being unready for prayer to be answered. Zechariah was rebuked, and became dumb and deaf for a while (as 1:62 implies).

Now Luke returns to the same theme, in one of the parables of Jesus. The main point is put first: **people ought always to pray and not lose heart** (18:1). Then comes the parable, which makes the point more forcefully. There was a judge in a certain town who cared nothing for God nor for anyone else. There was also a needy widow who asked him for legal help. The judge cared nothing about the woman's needs, nor was he a devout person at all, but the sheer persistence of the woman made him eventually give in to her request (18:2–5). After the story Jesus presses home its lessons.

1. **Persistence**. The judge was unjust and unwilling to help the woman. God is just and willing to help His elect, His chosen people. If the unjust judge responded to persistence, God will respond even more to the persistence of His people in prayer. It is an argument by way of contrast. If an *unjust* judge will help, a *righteous* God will do so even more. Widows

71

are people who are generally needy and defenceless. God's people are in a similar position. Often in the face of the world's wickedness, they need God's intervention on their behalf. They need God to 'come' in unexpected ways to rescue them in their plight.

It is easy to give up in prayer, but this displeases God. He wants us to persist. We may abandon prayers that we know are wrong. We may abandon a particular prayer if God tells us to stop (see Jeremiah 11:14), or if He has told us the answer is 'no'. But otherwise God wants us to persist. However long God may delay, if the prayer is good and right, we should persist in it until we have definite reason not to do so.

2. **Vindication**. Jesus says that God's people will experience His 'vindication' amidst injustice and oppression, if they will persist in prayer. *'And will not God bring about the vindication of his elect who cry out to him day and night?'* (18:7). 'Vindication' is being proved to be right. It is when something that is attacked or criticised is then proved to have God's approval. Jesus assumes that His people will often be in situations of injustice, like the widow of the parable. But He also assumes that God's elect will cry out to Him. One of the marks of salvation is prayer. God's elect pray! In answer to prayer God likes to demonstrate and make visible the sincerity and righteousness of His people. *'He will bring out your righteousness as the light'* (Psalm 37:6). He will uphold our cause when we are truly in His will. David said, *'The Lord has upheld my cause against Nabal'* (1 Samuel 25:39), and we shall be able to say the same, as long as we stay in God's will, endure the trials He allows to come upon us, and cry out to Him day and night.

3. **Timeliness**. Jesus says, *'I say to you, He will bring about their vindication speedily'* (18:8a). When God's people are in difficulty, one aspect of their troubles is that God seems to be slow to come to their aid. But God is never too late with His help, and He is never too early either! He sends His vindication at just the right time, at the time which will bring honour to His name and appreciation of His mighty sovereignty. It is not always as soon as we might wish, but it never comes too late. When God's vindication does come it is swift. He brings

about our vindication 'speedily'. God's people often cry out, 'Lord, how long?' (Psalm 6:3; 13:1; 35:17, and often elsewhere). 'How long must I call for help?' said Habakkuk (Habakkuk 1:2). But God is no slower than He has to be. He always says to us, *'He who is coming will not delay'* (Habakkuk 2:3). Although we may be impatient for His answer, when it finally comes we shall see that the delay was necessary and that God had His own reasons for it. But eventually He brings about vindication speedily.

4. **Readiness**. The question is: when God seems to delay, will we go on believing that He is on His way? *'When the Son of Man comes, will he find faith on the earth?'* (18:8b). This is not a statement about the 'Second Coming' of Jesus at the end of the world. Jesus has been talking about prayer. And before that He had been referring to 'comings' of Jesus in such events as the fall of Jerusalem. In the context of Luke 17:20–18:8 the 'coming' of Jesus refers to any event in which He 'comes' to vindicate His people and answer their prayers. This was the mistake that Zacharias made (1:5–25). He was not ready for God to 'come' to answer His need. When God did come, Zacharias was unready. God wants us to pray and not give up, to pray and then be full of faith when He comes.

# Chapter 22

## Experiencing God's Kingdom
### (Luke 18:9–17)

In the two stories here (18:9–14, 15–17) we are presented with two qualities that are necessary if we are to be acceptable to God and experience His kingdom.

1. **The first is humility**. The parable of the Pharisee and the tax collector is still continuing the theme of prayer and explains how we can be accepted by God. The worse thing to do is to try to stand before God in your own righteousness (18:9). We are to be persistent and daring in our prayers (18:1–8) but we cannot stand before God in any way except through His mercy.

Consider **the man who was not accepted by God**. (i) He tried to pray. There is nothing wrong with that! It is good to seek to pray. (ii) He honoured God's temple. (iii) He lived a moral life. (iv) He lived a disciplined life; he fasted. (v) He lived a generous life; he tithed. So far, so good. We cannot criticise any of these things. Yet he was not accepted by God! He was such a 'good' man, and yet God would not accept him. He was making one supreme mistake: **he was trying to stand before God in his own righteousness**. God hates self-righteousness. No 'good works' of our own entitle us to stand before God. Our good works are not good enough. The standard God sets is for us to be as pure as Jesus Himself. Our repentance is never sufficiently pure to entitle us to stand before God.

Self-righteous people are actually self-centred. Look at how much the Pharisee talked about 'himself'. 'I thank you that I am not like other people ... I fast ... I give tithes ...'.

Self-righteous people have a critical spirit. They despise others. Only before we have come to realise our own sinfulness can we talk about how righteous we are, and this leads us to feel that others are inferior. A critical spirit is a sign of self-righteousness.

Self-righteous people are not accepted by God. The man in the story was never accepted by God. He was only praying 'with himself' (18:11).

Consider **the man who was accepted by God.** (i) He was ashamed of himself. He stood a long way back from the temple gates. He was too ashamed to look up to God. (ii) He said nothing at all about his good works. (iii) He was distressed about his sins. No one repents perfectly – but this man was truly sorry for the way in which he had lived. (iv) He had faith. He was coming to God. He was praying. He did have hope of mercy. If he had not had faith, he would never have been received by God at all. (v) He asked for mercy – and he received it.

Jesus says this man was 'justified'. This is the favourite term of the apostle Paul, but we find it here in the words of Jesus. Perhaps Paul thought of talking about being 'justified' because he knew this story. To be 'justified' means to be 'declared righteous'. When the sinner comes in faith to God through Jesus, he is 'declared righteous' before God. It is not his own righteousness. It is a God-given righteousness. It is not **in** him; it is **covering** him. New birth and God's work of sanctification work righteousness **in** us. Justification is a covering righteousness which enables us to stand before God. Righteousness **in** us is always imperfect; Christ's righteousness **covering** us is perfect.

2. **The second is persistence in childlike faith.** Our first faith is needed if we are ever to be accepted by God at all. But something else is needed. If we are to fully enter into all that God has for us we must regularly and persistently have childlike faith. What are children like? It is a mistake to think they represent innocence. People who think that have presumably not known many children! But children do represent powerlessness; and they do represent trust. It is the latter that is relevant here. People were bringing young children to Jesus,

believing that if Jesus touched them they would somehow be blessed (18:5). The disciples did not want Jesus to be bothered in this way (18:15b) but Jesus wanted to see them. He liked to be directly in touch with people, including the children (18:16). At the same time Jesus took the opportunity to teach something. He was concerned for people to experience the kingdom of God. 'Entering the kingdom' means experiencing God in His royal power. To know God's kingdom-blessing requires **receiving** what Jesus has to give in simple faith. In practice it simply means believing and trusting what He says to us. Children are trusting. They generally believe what you say without getting too complicated. Christians are to be the same: believing what God says without getting too complicated.

Actually in the story of the Pharisee and the tax collector, the tax collector could have done with more of this simple childlike faith. Jesus tells the story to show that even someone in distress and grief over his sins can find peace with God. Yet actually the tax collector did not need to stand far off! He could have drawn near through bold and confident faith. His sins did not have to keep him 'standing some distance away'. *'Draw near with confidence,'* says the letter to the Hebrews (4:16). This is why persistent childlike faith has to become the characteristic of our life. It will first give us boldness in prayer. It will sustain us amidst trouble and bring us to steadfastness in times of testing. It will bring us to love amidst criticism and calmness when things are moving slowly for us and for God's kingdom. We shall enter the kingdom of God.

# Chapter 23

## The Rich Ruler

(Luke 18:18–30)

A ruler asks Jesus a question. He calls Jesus 'Good teacher' and, before the ruler has a chance to ask his question, Jesus holds up the conversation to talk about 'goodness'. The ruler is speaking rather flatteringly and Jesus uses the occasion to teach something about Himself. The gospels always give only compressed summaries of what they report. Here we presumably have only a summary of what was originally a lengthy conversation. Matthew tells us that the conversation also involved a discussion of 'doing some good thing' to inherit God's blessing (see Matthew 19:16–30). Mark's Gospel and Luke's Gospel tell us about the discussion of Jesus Himself (see also Mark 10:17–31). Our concern is Luke's version. Quite likely the original conversation included a good deal of talk about goodness and what it involved.

1. **The ruler is invited to think about Jesus Himself.** He begins in this flattering way, *'Good teacher . . .'*. Jesus is known for His goodness and kindness. The ruler draws attention to his admiration for Jesus by the way in which he speaks to Him. But has he thought much about this? It is true that Jesus is a genuinely good person. How many genuinely good people are there on planet earth? It all depends on how you think of goodness. But obviously Jesus is in a category all of His own. He is entirely unique in His kindness. There is no one like Him at all. *'Why do you call me good?'* says Jesus. It is an invitation to think more about Jesus **Himself.** The ruler wants a piece of advice from Jesus. The answer Jesus will give will include the requirement: *'follow me.'* If the ruler is to enter into everything

God has for him, it will mean getting involved with Jesus Himself.

2. **The ruler asks a question about 'inheriting'**. This is a vital word in biblical language. 'Inheriting' is more than justification by faith. 'Justification' is by faith only. The tax collector in Luke 18 was 'justified' (v. 14) without being told to do anything about the Mosaic law! The Pharisee spoke of matters mentioned by the law (adultery, tithing, 18:11, 12) but was not accepted by God. If the ruler of Luke 18:18 had asked, 'What must I do to be saved?' – referring to the earliest phrase of salvation – Jesus would have said something like 'Come to me, and have life' or would have told a parable like that of the prodigal son (Luke 15:11–32). But Jesus is being asked a much bigger question about 'inheritance'. 'Inheritance' is an altogether greater concept. It refers to reaping from God everything that He has to give us. Our 'good works' do come into this! Paul says that those who 'sow to the Spirit', by the way in which they live, reap back from the Spirit eternal life (Galatians 6:8). It is this 'reaping back' that is meant by the word 'inherit'. It is the same as having treasure in heaven (see 18:22) and it is the same as 'entering the kingdom' (18:23–25). The disciples call it being 'saved' (18:26) – but it is **reaping** salvation that is in view, the occasion when we inherit reward from God. This is clear from the way Jesus answers the disciples' question of 18:26. He goes on to speak of **reward**: receiving many times over the reward of houses or brothers or sisters or mothers or children or lands that have been left behind. This is not speaking of justification by faith only; it is speaking about reward that comes by living for God. This was the ruler's question in the first place.

3. **Jesus answers the question**. How do we enter into everything God has for us? Jesus replies that the young man must keep the law (18:20). He has done that, he says (18:21). Jesus does not dispute his keeping of the law, but he goes even higher than the law! The man must (i) go beyond the law and do things that the law never mentioned. Jesus has a special command for him that was never mentioned in the law of Moses. Jesus is asking him to surrender his wealth (18:22). It is not in the law of Moses, nor does Jesus ask this from

everyone. But this is what the young man is being asked to do. (ii) The young man must personally join Jesus' ministry-team. *'Come, follow me'* (18:22) is quite literal. Jesus wants the young man to abandon what he has been doing before and join Jesus in ministry. It will lead to the man's 'inheriting' – finding treasure in heaven.

4. **Wealth is a hindrance to inheriting God's purposes**. The young man is stunned (18:23). He had not imagined that Jesus would speak about abandoning his wealth. And he had never thought much about the **tenth** commandment! The ruler leaves Jesus, and Jesus gives a warning about wealth. It is almost impossible for anyone who is wealthy to enter fully into God's plans for their lives (18:24–25). This amazes the disciples. Who can ever get to the blessings of final salvation (18:26)? It takes the grace of God, says Jesus (18:27).

The event leads Peter to ask about the rewards that the disciples will receive (18:28). He is given encouragement. Those who have sacrificed material things for the sake of 'inheriting' the rewards of the kingdom will be abundantly rewarded in this life and eternally (18:29–30).

Wealthy people have to experience a miracle. Humanly speaking it is impossible for their wealth not to ruin their lives. But the things impossible with men and women are possible with God. The miracle is possible. God can give us such grace that we experience God's kingdom – but wealth does not help us in this matter!

# Chapter 24

## Seeing the Cross of Christ

### (Luke 18:31–43)

There is a connection between Jesus predicting His death and resurrection (18:31–43) and the healing of the blind man (18:35–43). Jesus is approaching the greatest event in the history of the world, the fulfilment of everything that was predicted and foreshadowed in the Old Testament Scriptures (18:31). This journey to Jerusalem will be Jesus' last, for He expects to suffer greatly and to be killed (18:32) and after that to be raised from the dead (18:33).

But the disciples find all of this entirely impossible and incomprehensible. They cannot believe that Jesus means what He says. They are totally bewildered by His predictions. *'They did not understand anything of all these things. This saying was hidden from them, and they did not understand what was said'* (18:34).

Immediately after this statement of the disciples' spiritual blindness comes the story of the gift of sight for the blind man. Jesus comes into the neighbourhood of Jericho. Actually he was going out of the city [1] but what happened in connection with Zacchaeus brought him back again (see 19:1, 5, 6). Since Luke tells the story of Zacchaeus which involves a return to the town it would not be appropriate to say 'as he was leaving Jericho' (as Mark 10:46 has it).

The miracles of Jesus are literal events, but they are also acted parables. The disciples' blindness has just been mentioned (18:34). They need to cry out to have their 'blindness' cured. The story of the healing is literal but it is also a parable and carries a lesson for us.

1. **We need to 'see' the cross**. The disciples had been followers of Jesus for three years. They were sincere people who had faith in Him as the Son of God and had been seeking to obey His teaching. And yet when Jesus spoke of His cross they were entirely blind. Jesus is about to fulfil everything that was predicted and foreshadowed in the Old Testament Scriptures (18:31), and yet they are blind to what is about to happen.

This is what the entire Scriptures were pointing to. Jesus is to be the seed of the woman who crushes the serpent's head (see Genesis 3:15). He is to be God's Passover Lamb, the fulfilment of all of the sacrifices of the Old Testament, the predicted Prophet, Priest and King. This is the central point of history – but the disciples do not see it and are not ready for it.

2. **It is necessary for Jesus to suffer**. He will be mocked and shamefully treated. He will be beaten and insulted. Jesus has to become a sympathetic Saviour. He must endure every kind of trial so as to be able to sympathise with men and women who suffer in similar ways.

3. **It is necessary for Jesus to die**. On the cross He will be bearing the sins of the human race. The Father will put upon Him the just penalty for the sins of the world. There can be no salvation unless Jesus pays the price of our sins.

4. **It is necessary for Jesus to rise from the dead**. A dead Saviour would be of no value to anyone. The human race needs a Saviour who has conquered death.

Jesus said to them, *'Behold, we are going up to Jerusalem ... Everything that is written ... will be accomplished ... '*. He gave them advance knowledge of what would happen – but they were blind. And it is in this context that the story of the healing of the blind man shows us what the disciples needed.

1. **The blind man knew his need**. Do they realise their need? Do they see that they are blind to what will be the greatest event in Jesus' life?

2. **The blind man was persistent in his request**. He heard that Jesus was nearby and started crying out, *'Son of David, have mercy on me!'* There were people walking ahead of Jesus who wanted to get him out of the way, but the blind man refused

to be discouraged. He knew what he wanted. Will the disciples be similarly determined to see what Jesus is saying about His destiny? The blind man was needy, but he was not lazy. He took steps to get his need met by Jesus. He took steps to make sure his request got to Jesus. People discouraged him but this did not hold him back. He was determined to get his sight given to him by Jesus. The disciples are blind also, not physically but in a spiritual manner. The eyes of their hearts are blinded. Will they be similarly determined to be cured by Jesus?

3. **The blind man knows of Jesus' Messiahship**. He knows that He is the 'Son of David'. Yet he wants something in addition; he wants Jesus to do His Messianic work of opening blind eyes. The disciples have also realised Jesus' greatness. They too know that He is the 'Son of David'. Will their eyes be opened to the fact that this mighty 'Son of David' must suffer and die, and be raised from the dead?

4. **The blind man gets what he wanted**. Jesus was compassionate. He stopped and found out what was happening. God likes to give us what we want! He also likes us to want the right things. So the man is healed by his faith. It leaves us with the question: will the disciples persist in their faith until they too have their eyes opened – in a deeper manner than the blind man ever experienced?

5. **The blind man glorified God**. When our eyes are opened, we see the greatness of what God does for us – and we give Him the praise.

## Note

1. See Eaton, *Mark* (Preaching through the Bible), Ch. 23, for comments on the three slightly different versions of this story in the first three gospels.

# Chapter 25

## Zacchaeus

### (Luke 19:1–10)

Jesus was passing through Jericho, about twenty-seven kilometres from Jerusalem. He did not intend to stay there long
(19:1). He was still heading for Jerusalem. But there was a
man in Jericho, named Zacchaeus, who very much wanted to
see Jesus. Zacchaeus was rich; he had got his wealth by a cruel
and corrupt method. He was a tax collector working for the
Roman government who occupied the land of Israel (19:2).

**God likes to lay hold of unlikely people and bring them to
salvation**. This is the story of a most unlikely convert!

1. **He is an unlikely convert because of what has happened in
his past**. These tax collectors had abandoned obedience to the
Mosaic law and to faith in the promises of a Saviour. They
worked for the pagan enemies of Israel. They had to be very
oppressive and severe men in order to get money out of
people. Zacchaeus was not the kind of person who was likely
to come to faith in Jesus.

2. **He is an unlikely convert because of what is happening in
his present life**. It does not seem very likely that he will have
any chance of seeing Jesus. He was small in height (19:3) and
so would not find it easy to get through the crowds – and no
one was likely to give him any help. Tax collectors were not
popular people in ancient Israel.

3. **He is an unlikely convert because of what will have to
happen in his future if he comes to know Jesus Christ**. If he ever
becomes a disciple of Jesus Christ his life will have to change
radically. His corrupt ways will have to end. He will have to
make some repayments to the many people he has swindled
and oppressed. Very likely he will have to give up his work

83

altogether. He would have too much to lose if he ever came to know Jesus. But the unlikely convert in fact comes to experience salvation!

**Let us see how this salvation came to Zacchaeus**.

1. **There was a desire in his heart for salvation**. How long it had been there we do not know, but there was a secret desire in Zacchaeus's life to meet with Jesus Christ. He was trying to see Jesus (19:3). When he found that he could not get to see Him, he did what was necessary to achieve what he wanted. He ran ahead of the crowds to a part of the road where he knew Jesus would come by. He climbed into a sycamore tree because he knew that Jesus would have to pass by that point sooner or later. He was making great efforts to get to see the Lord Jesus Christ. It seems that despite his wicked past God had been working in his heart, and he was wanting to know for himself what he had heard about Jesus Christ.

2. **He discovered that the Saviour receives anyone who wants salvation**. Zacchaeus evidently wanted to know more about Jesus, but I do not think he thought it very likely that salvation would actually come to him that day. But as soon as Zacchaeus took one step of faith towards Jesus, Jesus openly expressed that He received Zacchaeus into His kingdom. Jesus came by. God evidently revealed to Him that Zacchaeus was there, and that he was a man wanting salvation. Jesus looked up into the tree and said, *'Zacchaeus, hurry and come down; for I must stay at your house today!'* (19:5). What a surprise! The unlikely convert was wanted by Jesus. Jesus actually knew his name! Zacchaeus never dreamed that Jesus could know about him or want him. Salvation is always surprising. When we know what we are really like and then discover that the Saviour knows about us and wants us, it is always amazing!

3. **Zacchaeus was ready to respond to Jesus' invitation** (19:6). Salvation is by faith in Jesus. He believes that Jesus means what He said. Salvation comes to him immediately by simple faith in Jesus.

4. **Zacchaeus's salvation comes by God's amazing grace**. Zacchaeus finds that the people do not like salvation coming to him (19:7). I am not surprised. Zacchaeus was notorious

for his wicked ways. How could Jesus show friendship to such a wicked person? Actually, people do not like the grace of God. All of us are hard and severe. Even people who are naturally 'nice' are still moralistic and critical inwardly. No one by nature really likes grace. We all tend to dislike people like Zacchaeus intensely, especially if we have had to pay up because of their hard-hearted and oppressive ways. It is not surprising that the people intensely dislike this graciousness of Jesus towards Zacchaeus. But that is what Jesus is like. He is more gracious than we ever dream that He would be! Jesus does not even speak of repentance or the need for Zacchaeus to change his wicked ways. He simply welcomes Zacchaeus, even before he has made any changes in his life.

5. **Zacchaeus's faith was followed by a changed life**. His faith in Jesus led him to an amendment of the way he had been living. He was willing to do what he could to put right his oppression of needy people (19:8). This crooked person who was so disloyal to Israel was now a son of Abraham because he had come to the same kind of faith that Abraham had (19:9). This is what Jesus came into this world for: to seek and save the lost (19:10).

# Chapter 26

## Servants Faithful and Unfaithful
### (Luke 19:11–27)

People often think that the final glory of God's kingdom is going to come at any moment. In fact, we do not know when the end of the world might be. It certainly is good to be ready for interventions of God's judgement into our world at any time. But sometimes people get very excited about 'the last things' and like to insist that the end of the world must be very near, and will certainly be in our lifetime. People are quite sincere in this but it is not good to be over-dogmatic.

Jesus' disciples were among those who believed that God's glorious kingdom was very near at hand (19:11). However, Jesus told them a parable to persuade them not to expect an immediate glorious kingdom but to be prepared for a lengthy period of delay in which we are to serve God.

1. **The parable is a warning about delay** (19:12). A man of noble birth has to travel to a far-off land to receive a kingdom. Actually this happened several times in the royal family that ruled Israel. Various members of the Herod family who were the rulers of Israel had to travel to Rome to receive the power to rule from the Roman authorities.

This is a good illustration of what has happened in the life of Jesus. He has gone to the Father to receive a kingdom. Actually He has received His kingdom already and is ruling from heaven over the world. One day He will physically and literally return to reign as King more gloriously and visibly.

The main point is: the return of the King is delayed. The Father has reasons for wanting His Son to reign from heaven. He is the King of the universe but is physically absent from planet earth at the moment. The Second Coming of Jesus comes only after great delay. The delay has already lasted for two thousand years and may last even longer.

2. **The parable is a message to us about using the delay in Jesus' return** (19:13). In the parable, while the future king is absent he gives his servants some money to use in trade in the financial systems of Israel. Each has ten 'minas'; a 'mina' was a small amount of money. They are to use it to do business for the future king while he is away.

The parable is a picture of the situation of each Christian. We each have a 'measure of grace'. We have anointings and situations which we can use to serve our Lord Jesus Christ while He is physically absent from this world.

3. **The parable warns us that Jesus will call us to account for how we have served Him** (19:14–19). When the noble-man travels to the far-off country a separate delegation of citizens travels to the same far-away destination to tell the colonial rulers they do not want this man as king (19:14). This actually happened when Herod the Great died and his son Archelaus went to Rome to receive authority to be the next king. Fifty people from Israel also went to Rome to oppose his becoming the next king. There are people who say about Jesus, 'We do not want this man to reign over us.'

When the king returns he summons his servants to give account of how they have used the minas he gave them. The reward for having served the king is authority and the further privilege of serving him (19:15–19). When Jesus returns and finds that we have served Him, our reward will be the honour that He gives us. Perhaps also there will be varying levels in our authority as kings reigning with Christ. It starts even now. The more faithful we are, the more authority Jesus gives us.

4. **Those who are not fruitful will be punished** (19:20–26). One servant failed to serve his master, because he was paralysed by fear (19:20–21). The master calls his laziness wickedness and a sin against knowledge (19:22–23). The authority that should have belonged to the wicked servant is given to the faithful servant as an additional reward (19:24–26). Faithfulness gets **abundantly** rewarded; laziness gets punished. Lazy Christians will suffer serious loss, in this world and on the day of judgement.

5. **There are two kinds of punishment, one for disobedient servants and another for those who refuse to be servants at all** (19:27). It is to be noticed that lazy servants and complete rebels are considered separately and punished differently. As we have already seen, it is important not to try to get too much out of a parable, but it is clear the lazy servants suffer loss, whereas the rebels who refused their king altogether are executed. It will be similar in the final day of judgement. Lazy Christians will certainly suffer loss, and the loss will be terrible. But those who rebel even more seriously because they have rejected the kingship of Jesus altogether will experience the greatest punishment that can ever be known: what the Bible calls 'the second death'.

The important point of the parable is that Christians are each given their 'minas', their 'measure' of grace with which to serve God. The Second Coming of Jesus might be long delayed. We do not know for sure when He will return. It might be sooner than we think. But when Jesus returns He wants to find us busy using His grace, and using the various giftings and callings that He has placed upon us. Christians have certain things which we are to do for Jesus. When Jesus comes He will call us to account. There will be everlasting rewards for those who have served Him; there will be loss for those who have been lazy. To everyone who has served God, the privilege of doing more for Jesus will be given.

# Chapter 27

# What Sort of 'Jesus'?
## (Luke 19:28–40)

Luke's story now reaches Jesus' final approach to the city of Jerusalem. Still He is striding ahead of the disciples (19:28). He comes now to Bethphage and Bethany, two villages side by side on the outskirts of Jerusalem (19:29). Three attitudes to Jesus are visible in the story of His entry into Jerusalem.

1. **Jesus is loved by God**. God provides for Jesus' needs. Jesus sends two disciples to the nearest village, Bethphage, to fetch a colt for Him to ride (19:30–34). The story of the colt has been interpreted in various ways. Has some kind of prior arrangement been made, with the words 'The Lord has need of it' as a kind of password? No; the fact that the story receives special attention suggests that something miraculous is happening here. It seems that both Jesus and the colt's owners have been given miraculous guidance from God. 'The Lord' refers to God the Father (Jesus was not generally called 'the Lord' during His lifetime). It is like the story of Peter and Cornelius who both received divine guidance (Acts 10:3–6, 9–16) and so were miraculously brought together by God. The implication is that God is giving Jesus special help at this crucial time of His life. He needs an ass's colt to fulfil prophecy (see Zechariah 9:9). God provides what is needed, giving miraculous guidance both to Jesus and to some sympathisers in the suburbs of Jerusalem.

What is also unusual here is that no one has ever ridden the colt before (19:30) and, therefore, it is likely to be badly behaved with its first rider. This means that Jesus will be getting supernatural help as He rides into Jerusalem on an untrained colt. The disciples put cloaks on the colt and Jesus rides into Jerusalem (19:35).

2. **Jesus is misunderstood by His disciples**. Jesus' disciples honour Him as He enters Jerusalem, but as they do so they are full of misunderstanding. Jesus rides into Jerusalem in a very public way. The leaders of Israel will never have an opportunity to claim that they had no chance to receive Jesus. Jesus had often avoided publicity but now He knows that the time for avoiding publicity has finished. The common people claim to be Jesus' disciples and receive Him as a hero. They throw their cloaks on the ground making a kind of royal carpet for Him to ride along (19:36). The leaders of Israel will reject Jesus but He has many disciples and supporters among the ordinary people of Jerusalem. The common people think Jesus is some kind of Messiah, and it is clear that the leaders of Israel believe that Jesus is claiming to be Israel's king and messiah.

The disciples have a rather misguided idea of Messiahship. They still think that Jesus will be a political Messiah, who will save Israel from their colonial oppressors, the Romans. The people love the idea that Jesus is the Messiah but they have a completely wrong idea of what the 'Messiah' is. However, many of these people are true disciples. Even the twelve apostles thought that Jesus' Messiahship was political and earthly. James and John wanted to be leading personalities in the new state of Israel that they believed was coming (Mark 10:35–37). Even after the resurrection Peter was still hoping for something very political (see Acts 1:6).

It still happens. People think that Jesus will be a social reformer or a moral advisor or even a prayer-answerer who will help them pay the rent. Jesus can be all of these things but we have not seen Jesus rightly if this is all we see.

Many of these admirers of Jesus would be deluded by the religious leaders of Jerusalem within a few days. Now they were praising God for His miracles (19:37) and crying out, *'Blessed is the king who comes in the name of the Lord.'* They thought He would bring *'Peace in heaven and glory in the highest!'* God Himself is at peace because His King comes to Jerusalem. However, we must not try to interpret these words too exactly. They are not being used by scholars but by the ordinary people of Jerusalem. In a few days' time these same people would be crying, *'Crucify him! Crucify him!'*

It does not matter why we first come to Jesus, but as time goes on it must become clear to us that Jesus comes to save us from our sins. It is only **this** Jesus of the Bible who is the Saviour. 'Jesus' the rescuer of Israel from Roman colonial oppression was not the real Jesus at all. If, as Jesus makes it clear who He is, we accept Him for who He is, all is well. But if, when we find out more about Jesus, we do not want Him after all, then the Jesus we claimed to believe in never was the Jesus of the Bible. In times of testing many fall from what at first seemed to be faith in Jesus.

3. **Jesus is rejected by the leaders of Israel**. If the common people misunderstand Jesus but (for the moment) welcome Him, the leaders of Israel misunderstand Jesus and reject Him. The Pharisees are filled with jealousy. They hate the idea of Jesus receiving such honour. They want Jesus to rebuke His disciples, but He will not do it (19:39). The disciples' praise might be misinformed but their heart is right. He is indeed the Messiah. He has arrived in Jerusalem as its Saviour. Jesus uses a proverbial expression taken from Habakkuk 2:11. If men and women will not praise the Saviour as He arrives in Jerusalem, the city of salvation, then the very stones will cry out in protest.

# Chapter 28

# Lost Destiny

(Luke 19:41–48)

As Jesus approaches Jerusalem He breaks down and begins to weep (19:41). The leaders of this city will reject Him and will crucify Him. He knows that the city will come under the judgement of God.

1. **The story of Jerusalem is an example of a lost destiny**. God had promised that it would be 'out of Zion' that salvation would go to the world. Yet the city and its temple had lost sight of its wonderful destiny and was full of corruption.

The temple had a dramatic history. Solomon had built it, but God had always given warnings that if the people of Israel turned to sin, the temple would be destroyed. In 587 BC that is what happened. The glory of God was withdrawn, and the temple was destroyed by the Babylonians. Another temple was built about seventy years later in 515 BC, but this was not as big as the original one and the glory of God never returned in the same way. In about 20 BC Herod the Great started enlarging the second temple. The temple symbolised the holiness of God and the way of access to Him by the blood of sacrifice.

Jesus honoured the temple and regularly went to its festivals. During the last week of His life He spent much time teaching in its courts. Even after the resurrection of Jesus the disciples still honoured the temple (see 24:53; Acts 2:46). But Jesus wept over Jerusalem as He approached the city because He knew that it had lost sight of its destiny. It would still be the centre of salvation because Jesus died there and the Spirit was poured out on the Jerusalem church. It was from

Jerusalem that the gospel went out to the uttermost parts of the earth. Yet Jerusalem's destiny was being fulfilled only by a remnant. The vast majority of its inhabitants would reject the gospel and suffer in the terrible invasion of the city in AD 70.

This temple had been taken over by people buying and selling pigeons for the sacrifices, and no doubt other things as well. The entire place had become spiritually dead and traditional. Jesus gave the temple an opportunity to welcome Him, but He always knew that its worshippers would reject Him. They were **forgetful** (no longer keeping in mind the purpose of the temple), **blind** (unable to recognise Jesus), **unbelieving** (without faith in the promises of God concerning the city) and **corrupt** (twisting the use of the temple to their own selfish purposes).

It often happens that something which was truly used by God in days gone by gets to be misused. The temple was a picture of any place which God specially indwells. It can picture Christ (because God indwells Christ). It can picture the church (because God indwells the church). It can picture heaven, the dwelling place of God. And it can symbolise our own lives (because we too are to be temples of the Holy Spirit).

2. **Consider, next, the spiritual blessings the temple leaders were about to lose**. Jesus is weeping because He can see what is going to happen to this city with its temple. As He weeps He says, *'If only you, you also, had know today the things that make for peace. But now they have been hidden from your eyes'* (19:42).

**Jesus wanted them to have peace**. The temple was built at a time of peace. God would not let David build it because he was a man of war. The name 'Solomon' has a connection with the word for peace (*shalom*). If only they would receive Him, it would bring them the blessings of peace: peace with God, peace with each other, peace of conscience, and peace amidst the circumstances of life.

**Jesus wanted them to have understanding**. He says, 'But now they have been hidden from your eyes.' The people of Israel are unable to detect what is happening. The Son of God is visiting them, but they do not see it.

**Jesus wanted the protection of the next generation**. He could see into the future, and was concerned about the next generation. Forty years after His death the temple would be destroyed. He knows Israel's enemies will come (19:43) and the city will be destroyed. He says that they *'will level you to the ground, and your children within you, and they will not leave in you one stone upon another . . . '*.

**Jesus wanted His temple to be a place of prayer**. The temple was intended to symbolise the way to God, through the blood of a sacrifice for sins. It was intended to be a place where people gathered together in the courtyards for prayer. But the leaders of the temple were misusing it. Jesus throws out the sellers and small-time business people (19:46) and protests against what has happened.

**Jesus wanted His temple to be a place of teaching**. This is how Jesus is using the temple during His last few days on earth (19:47). The common people are listening, though the leaders of Israel are looking for a way to kill Jesus (19:48).

3. **There was only one sign of hope for Jerusalem and that is that Jesus was weeping**. It means that Jesus still loves the people of Jerusalem. He goes on teaching them, because some might listen to Him. Despite the majority who will reject Him, He goes on teaching because there might be a remnant who will trust Him. Three thousand people were converted in the city of Jerusalem on the Day of Pentecost. Jesus' tears and prayers brought some forward progress in the kingdom of God. Perhaps Jerusalem will again be used in the purpose of God. I would like to think so.

# Chapter 29

## Authority

(Luke 20:1–8)

Jesus has arrived in Jerusalem for the last time. The common people of Jerusalem have received Him warmly believing that Jesus is a political Messiah who will deliver them from the oppression of the Romans and raise Israel to eminence among the nations. The religious leaders hate Him.

Jesus has only a few days to live. He arrived in Jerusalem on a Sunday; He will be crucified on the Friday. The religious leaders are doing their utmost to get Jesus into trouble with the people. As Jesus is teaching in the temple, the chief priests, the scribes and the elders come to do what they can to oppose Him (20:1).

Their first question is a question of authority. Jesus had ejected the salespeople from the temple. They had turned a prayer-centre into a kind of religious market. They were making business out of the centre of Israel's system of worship. Now He is teaching the people. So the leaders of Israel ask the question: 'By what authority are you doing these things?' (20:2).

1. **We can see here two kinds of authority**. The chief priests, the scribes and elders have official authority, but they have no spiritual authority. They do not have the power of the Holy Spirit, but they do have a position of power within the religious organisation of the temple in Jerusalem. On the other hand, Jesus has spiritual authority but He does not have any political power. The Holy Spirit has anointed Him to preach. The power that came upon Jesus at the time of His baptism is still with Him. The people of Jerusalem can feel it as Jesus teaches and preaches. He teaches 'as one who has

authority and not as their scribes' (Matthew 7:29). The very
scribes who are interrogating Jesus have a certain amount of
official power but they know nothing of the power of the Holy
Spirit.

2. **The religious leaders have no interest in spiritual authority**.
They are asking a question about authority but they actually
have no real interest in the subject. If Jesus began to talk to
them about the authority of the Holy Spirit, they would only
use what He said against Him. Their reason for asking the
question is not because they want to know the answer but
because they hope Jesus will say something that will get Him
into trouble. If He says, 'I have authority because I am God's
Messiah', they will be able to claim that Jesus is a threat to the
Roman government. So they hope that Jesus will give an
answer that they can use to get rid of Him.

Their insincerity is soon revealed when Jesus answers their
question by asking them a question. 'Was the baptism of John
from heaven or from men?' (20:4). It is a good question to
ask. Jesus' authority was the same kind of authority that John
had. It was authority from God, authority that came upon
John because he was full of the Holy Spirit.

They refuse to answer the question. They do not really
believe in the kind of authority that John had, but they are
afraid to say so because the ordinary people of Jerusalem
recognised him as a man of spiritual power. They are afraid of
the people, and in that they reveal that they have no spiritual
authority. A man endued with the power of the Holy Spirit
does not live in fear of what people think of him. He leads the
people; he does not fear the people. The religious leaders of
Jerusalem reveal that they have no real authority at all. They
may have important positions in the religious hierarchy of
Jerusalem but they have no power to influence or bless the
people.

So they lie. They 'answered that they did not know where
John's authority came from' (20:7). Jesus brings the conversation to a close: 'Neither will I tell you by what authority I do
these things' (20:8). Jesus is not obliged to answer them. They
have themselves claimed that it is possible to say, 'We don't
know'. Why should Jesus answer a question about Himself

that they cannot answer about John. We are not obliged to give answers to interrogators.

3. **True authority comes from God**. The reader of Luke's Gospel knows where Jesus gets His authority from. At the beginning of Jesus' ministry the Holy Spirit came upon Him and has remained with Him ever since. His understanding, His miracles, His preaching, His great wisdom in answering questions – they all come from the power of the Holy Spirit which rests upon Him.

He has the authority of being sent by the Father to do His work. He was sent to seek and to save the lost. There is no greater authority than being in the will of God and responding to the call of God.

The question that might be asked of these religious leaders is: what is **their** authority? They have managed to get themselves into important positions in the leadership of Israel but what real authority do they have in the things of God. Has God commissioned them? Have they become aware of the power of the Holy Spirit in their lives? What authority do they have? They are able to lord it over others because they have managed to get themselves into some kind of official position within the leadership in Jerusalem. What kind of authority does Jesus have? The same as John: the power of the Holy Spirit coming upon someone sent by God to do His will.

# Chapter 30

## The Stone That the Builders Rejected
### (Luke 20:9–19)

The religious leaders of Israel hate Jesus; so Jesus now tells a parable that explains what is happening. A man plants a vineyard and rents it out to tenants (20:9). Many farms in first-century Israel were rented out by absentee landlords. Sometimes the tenants might try to seize the property for themselves. In the parable, the owner of the farm sends servants to see what is happening but each of his servants is ill-treated (20:10–12). Then he sends his son (20:13), but the tenants plan to kill him (20:14–15a). The owner of the vineyard is likely soon to destroy the tenants and rent out the vineyard to others (20:15b–16).

Seven points in the parable represent what was happening in the last week of Jesus' life. (i) The one who plants and owns the vineyard is God the Father. (ii) The vineyard is the people of God, 'Israel'. (iii) The servants are the various prophets and wise men who were sent to Israel. (iv) The son represents Jesus, the Son of God. (v) Ill-treatment of the son represents the murder of Jesus by the leaders of Israel. (vi) The destruction of the tenants represents the fall of Jerusalem in AD 70. (vii) The giving of the vineyard to others represents the progress of the gospel among gentiles.

After the parable Jesus presses home His message by using the words of Psalm 118:22 and Isaiah 28:14, 16 (20:17–19).

1. **Men and women have a tendency to misuse the church of Jesus Christ**. These leaders of Israel are like 'tenants' occupying someone else's property. God 'rented out' His business to the leaders of Israel but the tenants misuse it and want to use it to get profit for themselves. It is God's church, God's Israel,

and yet men and women like to use the church for their own ends. Perhaps the church, the people of God, might be called in to provide suitable ceremonies and pageantry on state occasions! And 'church leaders' take part in these great occasions but show no interest in preaching the gospel. Or in times of national emergency the churches will be asked to pray for the success of the government's policies! It is simply continuing what happened in ancient Israel. The high priests and elders of Israel had grabbed the use of the nation for themselves. They were in residence at the temple head-quarters. They got profit from the various pigeon-selling businesses that were occupying the courts of the temple. The 'tenants' were misusing the Landlord's property.

2. **It is a dangerous thing to ill-treat the Son of God because of personal earthly ambitions**. God sent servants to His 'vineyard': people like Obadiah, Joel, Hosea, Amos, Isaiah, Ezekiel and Jeremiah. They spoke of the coming Son of David and the coming outpouring of the Holy Spirit. They predicted the day when God would send salvation to Israel. But the prophets were always ill-treated. Jeremiah was imprisoned. Some prophets were killed.

But it is one thing to treat a prophet badly; it is yet more serious to ill-treat the Son of God. In the parable the owner of the vineyard sends servants, and then he sends his son. Similarly God sent various prophets and teachers to Israel, but now He is sending His beloved Son. These chief priests, scribes and elders are dealing with the Son of God Himself whom they are seeking to trap and get into trouble.

Just as ancient 'Israel' was very precious to God, so is God's re-structured 'Israel', the church of Jesus Christ. So Jesus warns – through His parable – that Jerusalem will soon be severely judged for its rejection of the Son of God. Jerusalem will be destroyed. God will re-arrange His 'Israel', pouring out the Spirit upon a few Jews and enlarging His church by adding gentiles, and will give His 'vineyard' to a new people for a long time.

3. **Jesus is a stone for building, or a stone for stumbling over**. Some builders go looking for a stone. They want a 'corner-stone', a large stone to be the main support in the foundation

of the building. **Jesus is unrecognised by religious experts**. Jesus is like a 'cornerstone'. You build your life upon Him. But these builders could not see a good stone when it was in front of their very eyes! Jesus, the Son of God, was walking around the courtyards of the temple but these religious experts could not see Him when He stood in front of them.

**Jesus is recognised by humble people**. There are a few ordinary people who see who Jesus is and build their lives upon Him.

**The stone that the builders reject becomes the most prominent stone in the entire building**. Soon Jesus will be crucified and then raised from the dead. The One the leaders of Israel rejected will become the Head of the people of God and the King of the universe.

**For those who reject 'the Stone', it becomes a means of judgement**. Like a heavy stone that falls out of a building and kills someone, soon this rejected stone will judge and destroy Jerusalem. Jesus is either a foundation stone or a stone that falls upon us in judgement. He is either received as a Saviour or faced as a Judge. The human race rejected Jesus; God exalted Him. The Christian sees now what everyone will see one day, that Jesus is the One chosen by God to be King of the universe and Saviour of all who trust Him. Religious leaders are strangely blind to Him, but for those whose eyes are opened He is the rock upon which their life is built.

# Chapter 31

## God and Caesar

(Luke 20:20–26)

The Jewish leaders pretend to be interested in Jesus. They have interesting theological questions that they want to put to Him. But it is all totally insincere. They hate Him, and want to murder Him (19:47). However, they cannot do what they want to do because He is so popular among the people and they are worried about public opinion (19:48; 20:6, 19b). They talk very religiously (20:21) but they know what Jesus thinks about them (20:19a). They have their spies out watching everything Jesus does and listening to everything He says, hoping He will say something that will get Him into trouble with the Roman authorities (20:20). Now they try to get Him to say something that they can report to the Romans.

It is strange that religious people have such an attitude towards Jesus. Religion is one thing; true love of Jesus and His gospel is another. Whether we are pleasing to God or not depends on our attitude to Jesus. These men are not seeing the glory of the Son of God who is among them. They want to ask their theological questions but are not asking the greatest question of all: who is Jesus? They are talking too much and listening too little. They need to stop the questions and listen to the Son of God who will teach them and save them if only they will listen to Him. They are preoccupied with small things (taxes!) and missing the big thing (Jesus!).

So these spies flatter Jesus (20:21) and then ask Him a question about the authority of the Roman colonial power. Should the Roman authority be recognised? Should the people pay taxes to Caesar, and so give recognition to the authority of the Roman power in Israel (20:22). It is an attempt to trick Jesus into saying something He should not say. If He says 'Yes', He will be recognising a pagan authority over Israel. That would break the Mosaic law (which demanded allegiance only to a Jewish king) and would displease the people, who looked for a Messiah who would remove the Romans. On the other hand, if Jesus said 'No, taxes should not be paid to Caesar', He could be taken to the Romans for punishment as a revolutionary.

Who is the authority in Israel? Is it God and the law of Moses? Or is it the occupying colonial power? Should they acknowledge Caesar's government by paying taxes to him?

Jesus answers by separating this world into two realms. Jesus could have refused to answer their question, but actually He did answer it. Although they were asking the question for bad reasons, the question was a good one and Jesus takes the opportunity to do some more teaching in the way in which He answers it. Jesus talks about church and state as two realms not one. He distinguishes between Caesar's realm and God's realm (although of course Caesar is under God). It is a very clever question, but it is only difficult if the view is taken that religion and state are to be unified. If Caesar is to be **religious** leader **and civic** leader, or if Caesar is to be rejected as **religious** leader and rejected as **civic** leader, then the question is difficult. The question assumes that a unified religion and state is necessary.

Jesus could see their deceit (20:23). He asks for a coin. Whose head is on it? Caesar's. They themselves are using Caesar's money! They themselves are already showing some respect for Caesar by using his money (20:24–25a). So – says Jesus – *'Give to Caesar what belongs to Caesar and give to God what belongs to God.'* They are astonished that He could answer them so skilfully (20:25b–26).

Jesus' answer separated loyalty to 'Caesar' and loyalty to 'God' and treated them as **two** realms. He held out the possibility of being loyal to Caesar and yet not being loyal to Caesar's religion. It was the first time in the history of thinking that anyone had spoken of religion and state as **two** realms. Before this it was generally accepted that Caesar was entitled to say which god should be worshipped (like Nebuchadnezzar in Daniel 3:1–6).

Religion and the state must be viewed separately. They have different memberships. All people within a given geographical area belong to the state, but not all citizens of that same area are members of the people of God. Christians are citizens of two realms. The functions of church and state are different. The state exists to be the servant of God in civic life. It keeps the peace among all the citizens and against outside enemies. But the church has a different function. Its primary calling is to be the 'pillar and ground of the truth', to proclaim our Lord Jesus Christ as the only hope of salvation. The church and the state have different weapons. The state 'does not bear the sword in vain'. The church has spiritual weapons.

The church and the state have different officials. The state has governors, magistrates, police officers, and so on. The officials of the Christian church are apostles, elders, deacons, and so on. The moment of entry into a nation is the time of birth. The moment of entry into the Christian church is the point of faith.

Christians are citizens of two realms. They belong to Caesar's realm: the realm of taxes, politics, education, health, welfare, and so on. They have a contribution to make to this aspect of life. Caesar has a certain amount of authority. He can demand that taxes be paid. But we are also to give to God the things that are God's: recognition, worship, faith, commitment.

# Chapter 32

# The Resurrection of the Dead

(Luke 20:27–40)

There were different groups of religious leaders in Israel. When Jesus was teaching in the courts of the temple during the last week of His life, all of the different kinds of Jewish leader were trying to get Jesus into trouble. Now the Saducees try to make Jesus look foolish. They ask a question about the resurrection of the dead.

1. **Resurrection is the greatest challenge to faith**. Here are **religious** people who are in power in the land of Israel. The Saducees were the denomination that had the greatest political power. Caiaphas was a Sadducee. They were worldly sceptical people, who despite their claim to be believers in the God of Israel had little faith in the supernatural. There are two different kinds of unbelieving religious people. Some are great lovers of church life but have no relationship with God – the Pharisees were mainly like that. Others are more interested in politics, morality and government affairs – this is what the Sadducees were like. Neither the Pharisees nor the Sadducees knew much about a personal relationship with God.

One of the greatest tests of true salvation is what you believe happens to you after you die. Do you believe in the resurrection of the body? It is quite a difficult thing to believe. Think about it! One day your body will have ceased to function and will begin to decompose. In one way or another God will raise your body. It is a great mystery but you will have a new body, and there will be some kind of connection between your new body and your old body. Quite how it all works I do not know, but your new body will resemble your old body in some way, and you will be recognisable. Do you believe in the resurrection of the dead? You either do or you don't. Which is it?

The Sadducees tried to ridicule the idea of resurrection by telling a hypothetical story (20:27–33). It is a rather silly story about seven brothers who all married the same woman one after the other, because each of the brothers died one at a time. It is based upon the 'Levirate marriage' in ancient Israel (in which if the husband died the widow was taken as wife by his brother). The question 'Whose wife will she be in the resurrection?' was designed to make the resurrection look silly.

2. **The hope of the resurrection is based on the faithfulness of God**. Jesus tells them bluntly they are wrong. They have an altogether wrong view of the after-life. There is no marriage in it (20:35), and there is no death in it (20:36).

He also rebukes them for their scepticism about the resurrection. The certainty of resurrection depends on God's faithfulness to His people. God has said that He is the God of Abraham, and the God of Isaac, and the God of Jacob. If the Sadducees were right Abraham, Isaac and Jacob were annihilated at the time of their death. But God speaks of Himself as still being in relationship with them.

It is very bold and daring to believe in resurrection. The Sadducees were governed by their scepticism but Jesus has a higher and greater view. The hope of life after death is rooted in God's faithfulness. God is faithful, and His relationship to His people continues after death. It is His faithfulness that guarantees He will reverse the processes of death and restore His people to life – and for Jesus this means life in a new body.

Many of the promises given to Abraham – for example that he would enjoy earthly territory and international fame – were never fulfilled in his lifetime. If God is to be faithful to Abraham and truly fulfil His promises to him, Abraham – and Isaac and Jacob – will have to be raised from the dead. Anyone with a real grasp of God's promises to Abraham and faith in His power will be able to see it that way. Abraham will have to be 'living' in a resurrection body for God to be completely faithful to him.

3. **Resurrection is connected with reward**. We notice that Jesus speaks of those who are *'considered worthy of taking part in that age and in the resurrection from the dead'* (20:35). This is a reminder to the Pharisees that resurrection is the occasion when people reap the results of what they have done in this life. The Sadducees want to put some awkward facts about resurrection. Well, Levirate marriage raises no problems, but the fact of judgement at the day of resurrection will raise far more difficult problems for these sceptical Sadducees. There is a resurrection to condemnation; some will be thrown into the lake of fire to be destroyed. Others will be 'worthy of the age of the resurrection which lasts for ever and ever'. Of course Jesus is not saying we come to the **first** phase of salvation by being 'worthy'. Good works will never be a way of justification. But good works are on the agenda for judgement day. The Sadducees expect to be annihilated at death, but Jesus warns them. They will survive long enough to face judgement and punishment. They will survive long enough to face exclusion from 'that age' – the heavenly kingdom where the righteous enjoy their heavenly rewards for ever and ever. They will survive long enough to repay every piece of wickedness they have ever committed. They like to think about awkward facts in connection with resurrection. Let them think about those awkward facts. There are no further questions for Jesus to answer after that (20:39–40).

# Chapter 33

## 'The Lord Said to My Lord'

(Luke 20:41–21:4)

The Jewish leaders have been trying to get Jesus into trouble. Now Jesus asks them a question.

1. **Consider Jesus**. Jesus is perfectly faithful. The New Testament describes Him as *'the faithful witness'* (Revelation 1:5). He knows how the Jewish leaders feel about Him. When He was walking towards Jerusalem He told the disciples several times that He would be ill-treated, betrayed and eventually executed. Yet He went to Jerusalem disregarding what might happen to Him. He was a faithful witness. He has been faithful in answering all of their questions.

Jesus will be faithful to you. The main thing He wants to talk to you about is Himself. We notice that the Jewish leaders want to talk about interesting theological questions, especially questions about the law of Moses. This is typical of a certain kind of person who wants to talk about morality or theological questions. But we notice the difference between their questions to Jesus and His questions to them. He wants to ask them questions about Himself. He asks them: what do you think about the Christ, the Messiah, the One who was foretold as the coming King of Israel? And He wants to know whether they are able to see in the Scriptures what the Messiah will be like (20:41–44). Of course, the Saviour is standing right there in front of them, talking to them. But somehow they do not see it.

Jesus wants to talk about Himself as the Son of God. He refers to Psalm 110. In Psalm 110, God's Saviour, the 'Messiah' or 'Christ' is said to be the 'Son of David'. Yet David speaks of his future son as 'My Lord'. How can this be?

How can a descendant of David be addressed as 'my Lord' even by David himself?

2. **Consider these people who are not at peace with God**. It is not difficult for a Christian to answer Jesus' question, but it was difficult for the scribes and teachers of the law in the temple at Jerusalem. People who earn their living from religion often are the last people on earth to know God. You would think these professional priests would have a deep understanding of the Bible, and that they would be very eager to find out everything they can about salvation and about knowing God.

People who are not at peace with God are the way they are because their eyes have never been opened to the Bible. People who are not at peace with God are the way they are because they have never really seen the Son of God. Who is the Son of God? He is 'Jesus' (20:41). He is 'the Christ' (someone who comes to rule over the entire people of God by the power of the Holy Spirit). He is the 'Son of David'. He is 'the Lord' even for King David! Even King David worships and admires the coming Saviour.

Jesus warns us against people that are religious professionals in some rigid denomination that claims to be speaking for God. Sadly, denominations decline. A group of people who are used by God at one time become a rigid inflexible organisation no longer following the Holy Spirit. Jesus tells us to be careful of such people. They are not likely to help us to know God. They like to be teachers. They like dressing up in special clothes. They love to be greeted as important people, with important titles. They like special honour in religious places; and they like special honour on social occasions (20:45–46). But they do not know God. They know a lot about professional religion, but they do not know God. And they like making money – even out of needy people (20:47).

**Consider one who is at peace with God**. Consider the next person in this Gospel of Luke, the widow who gave her two copper coins to the temple treasury. She is also in the temple like the religious leaders, but she is a very different kind of person.

1. She is poor and needy. God is often known far more by poor and needy people than He is by the rich and famous.

2. She is sacrificial. She had **two** coins, which means it would have been easy for her to put half of what she had into the temple treasury. If she only had one coin it is possible to see how the decision to put in everything might be almost forced on her, but with two coins this was not the case. She chose to do so.

Secret generosity is a good measure of spirituality. Pharisees like to get money (as in 20:47); those who are truly spiritual are generous and give sacrificially. The test of sacrificial giving is not how much you give but how much is left after you give.

So here are two types of people at the temple, the teachers of the law and the widows. The teachers of the law are there to get profit for themselves – including financial profit from widows. The widow is the very kind of person the experts in the law like to swindle. The teacher of the law is an expert in religious duty at the temple but he has not had his heart touched by God. It is easy to be busy in religious business and yet not touched by God's Holy Spirit. If the Pharisees had been touched by the Holy Spirit they would have had insight into the Scriptures, would have recognised Jesus as the One who fulfils Psalm 110 – and would have been generous like the widow instead of seeking to exploit her.

# Chapter 34

## The Fall of Jerusalem

(Luke 21:5–11)

When Jesus walks past the temple with His disciples they begin to admire the wonderful buildings (21:5). But Jesus is not very impressed with these wonderful buildings. He knows that what matters in the life of a country is not its wonderful buildings but whether that nation is full of people who will submit to Him and bow down to Him in faith. Jesus also knows something of the future of Jerusalem. He knows that the nation will reject Him. He has been predicting it many times as He journeys towards Jerusalem. He knows too that Jerusalem will come under the judgement of God. He tells the disciples: *'not one stone will be left on another'* (21:6).

How does He know such things? It is partly His knowledge of the Scriptures. He knows the Book of Daniel with its predictions of the fall of Jerusalem. And He has a God-given insight into the future by the Holy Spirit.

**It is foolish to admire the institutions of a country without reference to its morality and spirituality**. Here are these disciples admiring the wonderful buildings of Jerusalem. They look so beautiful. They look as if they will last a thousand years. But Jesus knows otherwise. He knows that what determines the well-being of a people is its faith in God, its spirituality, its morality, its integrity. *'Righteousness exalts a nation'* (Proverbs 13:34) –nothing else does! What made Israel great in the days before Jesus was the faith of a few of its leaders. What a mighty man was Moses who shaped and moulded the nation right at the beginning. What a great man was King David – despite his weaknesses. Israel had become a great nation under the leadership of these men. At the times in their history when they had fallen away from the law of Moses, they had fallen into periods of chaos. David had been a man after God's own heart; he had hated idolatry. There was no idolatry in his day, and he raised his nation to heights of greatness and influence. His son Solomon inherited a great nation because of the love that his father had for God. When the people had forgotten the law of Moses in the days after Moses, and when they had drifted into idolatry in the days **after** David chaos and destruction had come upon the nation. It is righteousness that exalts a nation, and nothing else.

Then there had been the days of Ezra and Nehemiah when God gave the nation another chance and – because of the nation's hatred of idolatry – Israel to some extent had become great again. Yet the nation had still not recovered the greatness it had known in the time of Moses and in the time of David. The people were longing for its prosperity to return.

Now – as we read in Luke's Gospel – Jesus has come to the nation. The people and leaders of the nation are being given an opportunity to respond to God as never before – and yet it is quite clear that they are not responding to Jesus in faith. As Jesus speaks and as the disciples admire these buildings, He has only a few days to live. He is soon to be crucified. The disciples are acting as if they are tourists admiring wonderful buildings but the crucifixion of Jesus is just a few days away! They are interested in the things that make Jerusalem famous and admired – and yet they have not taken much notice of Jesus' words concerning His fast-approaching death upon the cross. It is not great buildings that will preserve Israel; it is faith in God's Son. If the nation rejects God's Son the great walls and buildings of Jerusalem will be destroyed.

The disciples want to know more (21:7). They would like to know about the **timing** and the **signs** of the destruction of Jerusalem. Jesus answers their questions. There will come false Messiahs (21:8) and wars (21:9) but the end of the city of Jerusalem will not come as soon as they might think. Contrary to what people often believe, Luke 21 (and Matthew 24 and Mark 13) are **not** giving 'signs of the end'. Jesus is warning that despite great social upheavals the end is **not** going to be as soon as people might think. International conflicts will come (21:10), plus earthquakes and famines and pestilences (21:11). Even great signs in the skies will appear. The last few words of Luke 21:11 is Old Testament language speaking of a great change in events coming through the fall of a city (see Isaiah 13:10; 34:4; Ezekiel 32:7). Sometimes literal signs in the skies appear (as in Luke 23:45) even before the end of the world.

**Cities fall but the world continues**. The fall of Jerusalem is proof that Jesus has come to His kingdom. The generation after Jesus will see Jerusalem fall. But *'the end will not come right away'*. After the fall of Jerusalem will come a great time of opportunity for the disciples. About forty years after Jesus was crucified, Israel ceased to be a special people with institutions to enlighten the world. The Mosaic law ceased. The temple ceased to exist. Animal sacrifices ceased. Special holy days such as Passover time and the Day of Atonement ceased to be a part of God's requirement. God's kingly power in Israel was taken away. Jerusalem was destroyed. Jesus' words were fulfilled. Yet the opportunity for reaching the world with a message about Jesus was opened up as never before. Luke's 'Book of Acts' (only three chapters ahead in the two-part book Luke–Acts!) will tell the story. The end is not yet!

# Chapter 35

# Prophecy for Days of Tribulation
## (Luke 21:12-24)

Luke 21:12–24 is dealing with the period before the fall of Jerusalem when the disciples will go through difficult times. There is no reference to the Second Coming of Jesus before verse 25 and probably not even then. Unlike Matthew 24–25 and Mark 13, Luke 21 does not contain any teaching given at this time about Jesus' Second Coming. Luke is more concerned to report Jesus' words about the fall of Jerusalem. The reason for this is that the two-part book of Luke–Acts is interested in evangelism and in the part Jerusalem will play in the years of outreach after Jesus' death. The gospel will go out from Jerusalem (see Acts 1:8)! But Jesus' followers will have only one generation to get on with the work of preaching the gospel before Roman armies march on the city and Christians have to leave it (as 21:21 says will happen).

1. **Jesus gives them advice for enduring persecution**. There are four principles here. (i) Persecution will assist evangelism. The believers will often be arrested and persecuted (21:12) but this will help their evangelism! It will give them opportunities to witness to kings and governors (21:13). (ii) The Holy Spirit will help them in their witness (21:14–15). They will be given what to say when unexpectedly brought into times of danger mixed with opportunity. We recall how in the Book of Acts these words were fulfilled (see Acts 4:5–22; and the section that runs from 21:27 to 26:32). (iii) Great sufferings will have to be endured but the disciples will be kept safe amidst danger (21:16–18). (iv) Endurance will lead to great reward. *'By your endurance, gain your lives!'* says verse 19. 'Gaining life' refers to the rewards of God. It is not purely earthly survival

113

(because verse 16 warns that some might lose their lives, and most of the twelve apostles eventually were martyrs for Jesus). Nor is it 'getting to heaven' (because that is by faith in Jesus only). It is the full and rich life of the kingdom of God. God rewards us with a fuller and richer 'life' now; and we lay hold of the life of full reward from God in final glory.

2. **Jesus gives them advice for times when they would be able to escape disaster**. It is not always God's will that we stay exactly where we are when disaster comes. The Christians were to endure persecution for much of the time, but when it would become clear that Jerusalem was about to fall they had permission to escape. They were to run for their lives and avoid the terrible sufferings that would come when Jerusalem was about to fall (as happened in AD 70). They had asked about a sign (21:7). The 'sign' for escaping Jerusalem would be the sight of Roman soldiers. When the soldiers were seen approaching the city they would know that the end of Jerusalem had arrived (21:20), and that the city would no longer be a centre for evangelism for a long time to come. They should escape (21:21) for the sufferings of that period would be terrible (21:21–24). Jesus' words were fulfilled. The Jewish historian, Josephus, reported that over a million Jews were killed and 97,000 who escaped were sold as slaves. But the Christians escaped that 'great tribulation' because Jesus had told them what to do.

The phrase 'the times of the gentiles' (21:24) has interested interpreters of prophecy. Gentiles obtained control of Jerusalem in about 600 BC when it was invaded by the Babylonians. It stayed under gentile control until AD 1967 when the state of Israel gained full control of the walled city of Jerusalem. The idea in Jesus' prediction is that Jerusalem (from the viewpoint of the AD 30s) will not be given peace, and that after its fall it will be dominated by gentiles for a long time. The phrase suggests, however, that one day there will be a change and Jerusalem will again become a centre of spiritual blessing as it was in the days of David. I doubt whether 1967 was the fulfilment of these words. There has not been much peace in Jerusalem since 1967 and it has not become a centre of evangelism! Also it must be remembered that a person *'is not a Jew in a visible manner, nor is the circumcision that he has something in the open, in the flesh'* (Romans 2:28). Jewish people are generally without the inner circumcision of the heart. Spiritually, un-saved Jews are still gentiles! Jerusalem will go on being 'trodden down' until the nation turns to the Lord Jesus Christ. When Israel turns to Jesus (as Romans 11:26 suggests it will) Jerusalem will cease to be trodden down by gentiles and will become full of Christians. To say more than that, we shall have to wait for the event itself! The 'times of the gentiles' (21:24) is the period of Gentile domination, which I reckon is still going on despite the events of 1967.

What is important for us in all of this is that Jesus did not expect His disciples to be living lives of ease and luxury. There were dangerous days ahead of them, but Jesus did not tell them how to escape the dangers and live nice easy lives with good employment, plenty of comforts and nice holidays!

His great concern was reaching the nations with His message of salvation. The Christian life is not a matter of prosperity or playing around with religious rituals. The church is the agent of the kingdom! The disciples will have only one generation to mobilise evangelism from Jerusalem. Let them get on with the work of preaching the gospel before Roman armies march into the city.

# Chapter 36

# A Faithful Saviour

(Luke 21:25–38)

It is often thought that this section is about the Second Coming of Jesus, but actually verse 32 makes it unlikely that Jesus is speaking exclusively and directly of the Second Coming. I believe that the passage is dealing not with the Second Coming of Jesus directly but with the fall of Jerusalem as a **foretaste and anticipation** of the Second Coming. Luke's concern is specially with what is to happen in Jerusalem in the lifetime of the disciples, as verse 32 makes clear. The gospel will go out from Jerusalem, but they will have only one generation to get on with the work of preaching the good news before Jerusalem's final judgement from God.

1. **Jesus speaks of a fulfilment of Daniel 7:13** (21:25–27). There will be signs in the skies (21:25a), on earth (21:25b) and in the seas (21:25c), and terror among men and women at the calamities that are taking place (21:26). This kind of language is used by the Old Testament prophets to speak of massive changes in the history of the world. The shaking at the fall of Jerusalem is regarded as a convulsion in the cosmos, anticipating the cosmic shaking that will take place at the Second Coming of Jesus.

At that time – at the time of the fall of Jerusalem – *'they will see the Son of Man coming in a cloud with power and great glory'* (21:27). It must be remembered that the phrase 'coming of the Son of Man' does not always refer to Jesus' 'Second Coming'. In Daniel 7:13 the Son of Man comes **to** the Father to receive a kingdom. The outpouring of the Spirit, the progress of the church and the fall of Jerusalem were all ways

116

of seeing 'the Son of Man coming in the clouds', that is, seeing the fulfilment of Daniel 7:13.

The fall of Jerusalem is proof that Jesus has come to His kingdom. The generation after Jesus would see it themselves. 'Seeing the Son of Man coming in a cloud' does not refer to the Second Coming of Jesus but to the fulfilment of Daniel's prophecy. Daniel 7:13 gets fulfilled in stages. Jesus came to the Father to receive a kingdom. This takes place within the lifetime of His generation: (i) Matthew 16:27 (and parallels in Mark 8:38; Luke 9:26); (ii) Matthew 10:23; (iii) Matthew 24:30 (and parallels in Mark 13:26; Luke 21:27); (iv) Matthew 26:64 (and parallels in Mark 14:62; Luke 22:68). Matthew 26:64 speaks of it being true 'from now on'; so does Luke 21:27. Matthew 28:18 has the same idea (echoing Daniel 7:14); so does Matthew 19:28. The fulfilment of Daniel 7:13–14 takes place (i) in the resurrection and ascension of Jesus when He came to the Father to receive His kingly authority. It takes place (ii) in the fall of Jerusalem, when this striking judgement was seen, proving that Jesus was sitting on the throne of glory, and (iii) it is fulfilled in the visible 'Second Coming' of Jesus. Everything in Luke 21:5–24 plainly refers to the fall of Jerusalem; verses 25–36 continue the theme. These events are soon to take place, in the days of the apostles themselves.

2. **Jesus speaks words of encouragement** (21:28–33). 'Redemption' is drawing near at that time (21:28). A new phase of the kingdom is about to begin (21:29–31). The important point to note is: this will take place within one generation (21:32). Jesus' words are utterly reliable (21:33), so this will come about as He says. It will soon be 'summer time' (21:29–30), a time when many pleasant things take place. About forty years after Jesus was crucified, Israel ceased to be a special people with institutions to enlighten the world. God's kingly power in Israel was taken away. Jerusalem was destroyed. The first generations of the church were a time of great expansion and spiritual power. It was summer-time for the church but judgement day for Jerusalem.

3. **Jesus asks for soberness and readiness** (21:34–36). Jesus comes in more than one way. If it is not His final coming that we experience then it will be His coming in some other form.

We must not get weighed down with cares and anxieties, so that we neglect God (21:34). Sometimes Jesus can do something which although it is not the end of the world it is the end of our world. Sometimes He may come to take us to Himself. Sometimes He decides to 'take a look' at what is happening in our lives. He decides to investigate and reward or chasten according to what He finds.

4. **Jesus continues in faithful ministry for the people** (21:37–38). To the very last day of His life He does as much as He possibly can. The ordinary people of Jerusalem are eager to hear Jesus, and rise early every day to listen to what He has to say. There is a difference between the people (21:38) and the Jewish leaders. The leaders of the land want to keep their religious career just as it is, and get rid of Jesus, but they are afraid of the people (22:1–2). The people are soon to stumble and fall, but their fall will be the result of bad leadership. The 'shepherds' of the people are unfaithful. The people are willing to listen to Jesus, but are soon to be misled by the leaders of the land.

But Jesus continues in faithfulness to the very end. Like many others at Passover time He camps at night on the Mount of Olives near to Jerusalem. He is doing the right thing: teaching. He is in the right place: at the temple. He is faithful in the right use of His time: He is there from morning to evening. He is a faithful Saviour.

# Chapter 37

# Satan and Judas

(Luke 22:1–6)

Chapters 22 to 24 of Luke's Gospel tell the story of the death and resurrection of Jesus. They are among the most wonderful chapters of the Bible. God was planning that the cross of Jesus should be a Passover sacrifice (22:1–2). But the religious leaders wanted Jesus crucified before the festival time.[1] They were afraid of the people who would crowd into Jerusalem for the Passover and wanted to get rid of Jesus speedily. Then unexpectedly Judas comes to them to offer his help (22:3–5).

1. **Judas was a pretender**. He was a man who had claimed and pretended to be one of the disciples of Jesus, but he never was a believer. From the very beginning Jesus knew He was a betrayer. He was never 'clean' (John 13:10–11). He was not a 'backslider' (a Christian overtaken by some serious sin), but rather a pretender, a person who mixes with the disciples and claims to be one of them but has no faith. There are always those who find it convenient to pretend to believe what Christians believe. They can even join in God's work. They may even be used by God although Jesus has never known them (see Matthew 7:22–23). Judas was expecting Jesus to establish a kingdom of power and he wanted to get advantages for himself by being part of the new regime that he believed was about to bring. it. When Jesus made it increasingly clear that He was walking to the cross, Judas decided to change sides! He wanted to be on whatever side was most profitable to his finances.

2. **His sinfulness left him vulnerable to the devil**. There came a point when 'Satan entered Judas' (22:3). The devil comes and goes! In Luke 4:13 he left Jesus alone for a while but at

119

various times in His life the devil came back to attack the Son of God. There are times when it is the devil's hour (see 22:53) and he attacks God's Son or God's servants. When we are close to God we are safe. But sin leaves us vulnerable. Judas was full of ambition and greed. People like him are vulnerable to having demonic powers 'enter' them. Here Satan himself does the 'entering'. Judas has left the door of his life open (see Ephesians 4:27). He has no protective shield (see Ephesians 6:10–20).

3. **An imitation-church is at work in crucifying the Son of God.** I call the people here an 'imitation-church'. There are chief priests (those who ran the work of the temple) and scribes (the scholars and students of the Old Testament law). There is a specially religious occasion, the festival of Unleavened Bread and Passover. There is Judas, one of the apostles of the Lord Jesus Christ. There are temple officers, who looked after the treasury (22:4). You could call them the 'deacons' of the temple. There are discussions about what to do with Jesus and His rebellious apostle Judas (22:5). How religious people like committees and discussions about church business! It is a lot of people playing at the game of religion. Yet all the discussions and the financial transactions of these verses are with the intention of getting rid of Jesus.

The common people were totally left out of all this. They had no idea of what was going on. This is typical of corrupt religion. Church-leaders get into positions of power but have no interest in the gospel of the Lord Jesus Christ. The common people are used for the purposes of fund-raising but not much more.

True spirituality is the exact opposite. (i) It is sincere. It desires the honour and glory of the Lord Jesus Christ. It lifts high the name of Jesus. A false church is never very interested in the glory of the Lord Jesus Christ. (ii) True spirituality has the needs of the people at heart. (iii) True spirituality is content with God's will. What are the motives driving Judas and these religious leaders? Judas wants money. The religious leaders of Jerusalem want power to stay in their hands without anyone like Jesus coming and disturbing their careers in the temple! They are governed by self-centredness and money-making.

4. **Judas and Satan are being used without their knowledge**. These verses paint a terrible picture. Corrupt religious officials. A wicked and deceitful apostle. Satan getting hold of a man's heart and leading him into betrayal. Judas and his new friends watching for an opportunity to get rid of the Son of God. What a ghastly picture it all is!

And yet God was not being defeated. On the contrary God was getting His will done. Judas and his new colleagues were intending evil, but God was intending salvation! This is something we need to know about Satan. God uses Satan and wicked people even when they are doing their worst. God does not get defeated even when His enemies are full of deceit and betrayal of the worst kind. Satan was actually taking Jesus to the cross – but the cross was God's way of salvation. God can use evil. When the devil thinks he is getting his greatest victory, he is moving towards his greatest failure. We need to keep our eyes open for the way in which God overrules in the midst of terrible wickedness. When everything is going wrong, maybe everything is going right. When sin is at its worst – it can be used by God to achieve what God wants despite the wickedness of the people themselves. God may seem to lose a few battles, but He always ends up the Victor. He gets His will done, and neither Judas nor Satan can stop Him. They might even help Him without knowing it.

## Note

1. For the significance of this see Eaton, *Mark* (Preaching Through the Bible), p. 127.

# Chapter 38

## The Heavenly Banquet

### (Luke 22:7–18)

God had planned that the death of Jesus would take place at Passover time (Matthew 26:1–5; Mark 14:1–2; Luke 22:1–2). At some stage in the week Jesus had been anointed at Bethany (Matthew 26:6–13; Mark 14:3–9) and Judas had made plans to betray Him (Matthew 26:14–16; Mark 14:10–11; Luke 22:3–6).

Now Luke tells us that the 'day of Unleavened Bread' has arrived (22:7). It is the Thursday. The disciples are sent to prepare for the feast (22:8–9). Jesus will use an upper room in the city of Jerusalem (22:10–12). Either God had guided both the owners of the house and Jesus 'by the Holy Spirit' to be ready for each other (as I believe and as in Acts 10:1–23), or Jesus had made an arrangement to use the house of a friend but kept the arrangements secret so that He would not be arrested too soon. It was quite possibly the home of John Mark's parents in Jerusalem. The disciples get the room ready as Jesus wishes (22:13).

So the hour comes for the last meal that Jesus will ever have during His earthly ministry. His crucifixion is only a few hours away. He sits at the table (22:14) and tells them how important this last supper is to Him (22:15). *'I have very much wanted to eat this Passover with you before I suffer,'* He says (22:15). Why is this 'last supper' so important to Him?

**Jesus wants them to understand His death**. The Lord's Supper helps us to understand the cross. It makes us realise that the death of Jesus was a sacrifice for sin. It was not some kind of accident. It was the will of God for His Son Jesus, who was dying as a Passover lamb. Just as God 'passed over' the

122

sins of each family in which the firstborn took shelter under the blood of the lamb, so God passes over the sins of all who put their faith in Jesus and His blood.

**Jesus wants fellowship with His disciples before He goes to heaven**. Jesus was a man, a real human being. Although He was the Son of God, He was also a real human being. He liked to spend time with people. He enjoyed being with His disciples. Now, during these last hours of His life, He wants to be with His friends and fellow-workers. He wants to talk to them about the things of God. Many things were happening all in this short space of time. Jesus shared His words about love (John 13:31–35), gave a warning to Peter (22:31–34), told them about Scripture being fulfilled (22:37). The 'Farewell Discourses' start during this time (John 14:1–31a) and then continue as Jesus goes towards Gethsemane (note John 14:31b). Jesus wants to use this occasion to give last-minute help and instruction to His disciples. He is thinking of them to the very end of His life (see John13:1a). So He says, 'I have very much wanted to eat this Passover with you before I suffer.'

Jesus knows about His very imminent death but stays cool in trouble. He says, 'I have ... wanted ... this ... before I suffer.' He knows something of the great suffering ahead of Him, yet He is leaving Himself in the hands of God.

**Jesus knows that the last supper is prophetic**. The 'eating' will be 'fulfilled' in the kingdom of God (22:16). So will the drinking of the cup of wine. Jesus takes a cup and gives it to them. It is a foretaste of a banquet they will have in heaven (22:17–18).

**This gives us an idea of what heaven is**. Heaven is described in many ways. Among other thing it is like a banquet.

Heaven is a place of ease and comfort. The time for resting is not now in this life. There will be relaxation in heaven. Heaven will be a party, a banquet. At a banquet you relax in comfort while people bring food to you as you need it. Jesus brings us to His banqueting table; His banner over us is love.

Heaven is a place of fellowship. We will have time to sit and talk and share. There is a lot of 'meal symbolism' in the Scriptures. When we open our heart to Jesus He 'has supper' with us (Revelation 3:20). Heaven will be a place where we banquet with Jesus.

Heaven is a place of provision. Just as at a banquet the servers set good things on the table for us, so heaven will be the place where God finally and fully meets all our needs and continues to satisfy us for ever.

There is an aspect of the Lord's Supper that Luke specially emphasises. This is the first cup of Luke 22:17 (before the cup of Luke 22:20 which is different) which draws our attention to the fact that we are on our way to a heavenly banquet. At the Lord's Supper we have a foretaste of this heavenly banquet. We sit down in a leisurely manner with our Lord Jesus Christ and we have fellowship with Him. We share the joys of what He is doing for us.

The Lord's Supper looks forward to the Second Coming of Jesus because it reminds us that Jesus is absent, physically, from this world and that we shall not meet Him in His glorified body until the end of the world.

Eventually the final stage of the kingdom of God will come. When it finally comes in power the kingdom will be glorious and Jesus will be its King in a visible manner. Now the kingdom is working more quietly and is only slowly gaining victory over sin and darkness. But a day of final victory is coming. On that day we will enjoy a banquet with our Lord Jesus Christ.

# Chapter 39

# Eating, Betraying, Arguing
## (Luke 22:19–30)

As Jesus continues to celebrate the Passover with His disciples He now introduces what we call 'the Lord's Supper'. In this part of the story two people and a group of people each have their minds on different things.

1. **Jesus has His mind on the cross**. In just a few hours Jesus knows He will have died. He knows that in twenty-four hours He will be dead and buried. He also knows that His death upon the cross will be a ransom for many. It will be the means of salvation for all who believe in Him.

The Lord's Supper is a time for thanksgiving. At the Passover meal there was thanksgiving for the bread (22:19). Jesus' giving thanks is a hint to us that we are to give thanks for His dying for us.

The Lord's Supper is a symbolic meal. It began as a Passover celebration, in which the families of Israel would celebrate what God had done for the nation hundreds of years before. As a nation they had been saved by the blood of the Passover lamb.

Jesus takes bread and breaks it. The breaking of the bread symbolises the suffering of Jesus (22:19). Of course the breaking was necessary for the bread to be given out to the disciples, but the fact that it is mentioned probably means that there is more to it than that. Jesus was 'broken' on the cross. It is not that His bones were broken – that did not happen – but He was broken in suffering. The breaking of bread speaks of the way in which each person who eats it will participate in the benefits of the cross; and it speaks of the suffering of Jesus.

The bread itself is a symbol of the body of Christ (22:19). Jesus will bear the sins of the world in His body on the tree. 'Do this' means 'have a symbolic meal like this; and break bread and distribute it to the believers'. Its purpose is thanksgiving (as the first part of the verse suggests) and remembering.

The cup speaks symbolically of the new covenant (22:20). In the new covenant God relates to His people, gives us certain promises, and offers to confirm the promise by the taking of an oath. Every covenant has to take effect in direct connection with sacrifice. There can be no covenant without 'the blood of the covenant'. It is the death of Jesus for our sins that makes it possible for us to be in relationship with God. That is the 'blood of the covenant'. The wine speaks of the blood which keeps us in covenant with God and enables us to continue in obedience and faith until God swears the covenant oath and we inherit what He is wanting to give us.

2. **Judas has his mind on betraying Jesus**. Judas is a pretender. As we have seen, he has never been a true believer but has been deliberately play-acting, pretending to be a supporter of Jesus and a believer. He was not a backslider: he was a fake disciple. It is possible to be a hypocrite in the church: a person playing a part. Judas was a personal colleague of Jesus. He saw dozens of the miracles of Jesus and heard all His sermons, but none of this brought him to faith. Judas gets a loving warning from Jesus (22:21). Jesus lets His disciples know that one of them whose hand is on the table eating a meal with Him is about to betray Him. It is a warning to Judas and yet it does not expose him. Faced with this supernatural knowledge Judas ought surely to have realised that Jesus is exactly who He says He is, God's Messiah and Saviour. To disown Him and side with His enemies will be terrible evidence of unbelief.

Judas does not defeat the plan of God. Jesus will die according to God's plan, but the one who deliberately betrays Him will face terrible judgement. Human responsibility and God's sovereignty are present at the same time (22:22). God uses Judas to get the divine will done, but Judas is still willingly sinning. And Judas has no chance of defeating God.

Judas will not get his will done; he will be used in getting God's will done.

We note that Judas is not exposed by Jesus. The other disciples do not know who He is referring to (22:23). Judas betrayed Jesus, but Jesus never betrayed Judas. Judas betrayed himself.

3. **The disciples have their minds on earthly greatness** (22:24–30). Luke places the dispute about lordship at this point. The other gospels have it in a different position – perhaps it happened twice. More likely this dispute was continuing all the time. The disciples are interested in earthly greatness (22:24). Jesus does not criticise that. It is good to want to be great in serving God, but there is a right and a wrong kind of ambition. There is ambition for worldly greatness (22:25), which the disciples are not to want to have. They must be a contrast (22:26–27). They must be concerned about ministering to others as Jesus Himself is. Their reward will come in due course (22:28–30).

Different things were all happening at the same time. Judas was showing his wickedness. The disciples were showing their immaturity. But Jesus had His mind on the cross and His going there to be a Saviour for us. At the time when some were being wicked and others were showing immaturity, Jesus was showing faithfulness. The foolishness of others did not stop Him. Jesus was determined to be the Saviour of the world.

# Chapter 40

# Facing Great Changes
## (Luke 22:31–38)

The disciples are facing the greatest change they are ever going to experience. Jesus, whom they have known as a close friend for more than three years, is about to be executed. The disciples will be scattered. For a couple of days they will not know what is happening. Never will they have Jesus back with them in precisely the same way as before. Jesus has a word for these disciples of His, as they face the greatest upheaval of their lives.

1. **This time of change will be a time of danger**. Jesus says, *'Satan has asked to have all of you to sift you like wheat'* (22:31). The word 'you' is plural. Jesus is speaking especially to Peter but He is referring to all of the disciples. Satan wishes to 'sift' the disciples, to find out their weak points, to persuade them to sin, to encourage them to abandon their faith in their Saviour.

2. **Despite the greatness of the danger, Peter's faith will not fail**. Jesus is interceding for Peter and Jesus gets His prayers answered (22:32). We note that Jesus does not say, 'I have prayed for you that you will never be tempted', or '...that you will never fall'. Jesus' intercession guarantees the preservation of our faith. The true believer never entirely stops believing (although there may be many temporary failures). Despite what sin Peter might fall into, His Saviour preserves his faith. Jesus' intercession guarantees that we will continue to trust in our Saviour. Peter is very ignorant at this stage in his life, and entirely confident in himself (22:33–34).

3. **Jesus draws attention to His own faithfulness**. There will be many changes in the disciples' life after Jesus' death and

resurrection. At an earlier time in their lives, they had been sent to Israel. They were to look for support from the people to whom they ministered. They were told not to carry a purse or the provisions that they needed. Jesus promised that they would find their support through the people of Israel to whom they ministered. But now a change is about to come. They will no longer be ministering only to the lost sheep of the house of Israel. They are about to be sent to all nations. They will have to have a purse and they will have to carry some supplies with them. They will not be able to get their funds from the pagan nations to which they travel.

Jesus asks a question: did they lack anything when they were sent to Israel? No (22:35)! Nor will they lack anything in the future (22:36). They surely have discovered God's faithfulness already. The crucifixion of Jesus will be the point at which His ministry to Israel ends and His ministry to the nations begins (22:37). Under the old arrangements (no purse, no spare shirt, no staff provided by themselves), they had discovered that God was faithful and they lacked nothing. Under the new arrangements (carrying a purse, providing for themselves a sword, taking adequate resources), they will find God equally faithful. Changes are coming into their lives, but just as God was faithful before so He will be faithful to them again.

4. **The great changes that are about to come into their lives will lead them into fuller ministry**. Jesus knows everything that is about to happen. He knows Peter will deny his master. He knows that he will curse and take oaths and say, 'I know not the man'. But Jesus also knows that Peter will be restored. *'I have prayed for you that your faith does not fail.'* Peter's faith is indestructible. Jesus knows that there will be a time when faith fails, and He know that Peter will recover. *'When you have turned around, strengthen your brothers and sisters.'* Peter has been the leader of the twelve apostles (second to Jesus), and he will continue to be the leader of the church in its early days. It will be Peter who preaches on the Day of Pentecost.

We know what happened. Peter did indeed fail badly on the day when Jesus was arrested. He had said, 'I will never deny you', but it turned out that he did not know himself as well as Jesus knew him.

But Peter went on believing despite what he had done in denying Jesus. One look from Jesus brought him immediately to great distress. Jesus was praying that his faith would not fail. We remember how he was re-commissioned after Jesus was raised from the dead. God worked all things together for good. Peter found out things about himself that he never knew. He found out more of the faithfulness of his Saviour. Fifty-two days after he was cursing and denying Jesus he was present on the Day of Pentecost. The one who had betrayed his Master began to preach and three thousand people came to faith in Jesus.

God works in our lives by putting us through great changes. The disciples went through different stages of God's salvation and it caused different stages in their own lives. People who move on with God get pushed by God from one stage to the next in their story of serving Him. We do not exactly have to go through changes in the history of salvation, in the way the disciples witnessed the crucifixion of Jesus and the giving of the Spirit, Jesus is only crucified once. He is only raised from the dead once. There were some things that were unique about the Day of Pentecost. Yet the principles remain the same. Satan desires to sift us when he has special opportunities. Jesus ever lives to make intercession. He puts us through varied experiences in which, one way or another, we are able to strengthen our brothers and sisters.

# Chapter 41

## The Call to Prayer

(Luke 22:39–53)

Luke's Gospel, above all the other three, is the one that emphasises prayer.

**Jesus tells His disciples to pray** (22:39–40). Difficult days are ahead for them. They must pray so as not to enter into temptation. 'Entering into temptation' means coming under the power of temptation, so that you do something you ought not to do. We do not pray that we shall not be tempted – because all Christians will face temptation. Temptation cannot be prayed away! Jesus speaks of not being led 'into' temptation, that is, not being taken into a situation in which we are not able to stand.

The praying has to be done before the time of temptation. Often we find ourselves under pressure to fall or to sin in some way, and at that point we begin to pray, 'Lord, don't let me fall.' That is all right, but it is not quite what Jesus has in mind here. It is like the story of the boy who was healed of a evil spirit in Mark 9:14–29. Jesus had already been praying when He cast out the demon (note verse 29). Prayer is to be a **habit** and not only something we do in an emergency! We can all pray in an emergency (like Nehemiah in Nehemiah 2:4), but we do not always know when the emergency is going to come.

**Jesus prays Himself** (22:41–44). He did so as a matter of constant habit. We notice the words 'as was his custom' in 22:39. Jesus had had these times of prayer before. His praying is in privacy (22:41), and with reverence (22:42). He explores whether there might be another way of saving the world (22:42), and yet comes to see that there is no other option than

131

the cross. Your will be done', He says – knowing **now** that there is no other way open for him except the way of the cross. It is exploratory praying, and it is submissive praying. A revelation is given to Him as He prays; He sees that there is no way that the cross can be avoided.

Verse 44 shows us the greatness of what it cost Jesus to go to the cross. He began to feel the anger of God against sin. He was not afraid of a martyr's death; there was more to it than that.

Jesus' praying is answered but in God's way. The cup is not taken away but Jesus receives angelic help in drinking it (22:43).

**The disciples fail in their praying (22:45–46)**. Sleepiness leads to failure. These disciples were not aware they were in any time of crisis, but those who were about to arrest Jesus were already on their way! The crisis, when they 'entered into temptation', would come upon them very suddenly. They had been warned by Jesus but they were not ready for the sudden time of testing. It was 'while Jesus was still speaking' (22:47) that a crowd arrived to arrest Jesus. Jesus had been warning them that a special time of testing and tempting was just about to come. They should have been specially prayerful before such a time arrived, but now it has arrived! It is important to have times of prayerfulness. A good plan is to set aside time every day (an hour?), time every week or month (a morning? an evening? a weekend?), and a time in the year (over the new year?). I make no rules, but in one way or another we have to have time to pray in order not to 'enter' into temptation when testing suddenly comes.

**Judas arrives** (22:47–53). Perhaps the best way of considering these verses is to look at the five people or groups of people that are involved.

1. **There is the crowd**. They are relatively **ignorant**. I say 'relatively' ignorant because it is our responsibility to get to know God's will. Ignorance of His will is not an excuse that God will accept. On the judgement day we shall not be able to say, 'I did not know', because God will answer: 'But why did you not know?' We can seek to know God's will – and we ought to do so.

Yet we are slow to learn and God is patient with our slowness. A few weeks later Peter would talk to some of these people again under very different circumstances. *'This Jesus ... you crucified and killed by the hands of lawless men,'* he would say to some of these very people, the common people of Jerusalem, some of whom were there when Jesus was arrested. They came to see how ignorant they were and cried out in distress (Acts 2:37). Paul was once like this. He had opposed the gospel ignorantly and in unbelief (1 Timothy 1:13–16).

2. **There is Judas**. He is a different kind of person altogether. He is **a pretender**, getting into the small group of apostles because he thought he would be able to gain some advantage for himself.

3. **There are the officials**, who come to arrest Jesus. They are in official positions of authority and are **prejudiced** towards anything new. You should always feel slightly sorry for people in authority! When God is working and doing something unexpected, the ordinary people are often more open than those in positions of leadership and authority.

4. **There are the disciples**. They are characterised by great **weakness**. They are all just about to run away.

5. **Then – most important of all – there is Jesus**. What is Jesus doing? He is a faithful witness (Revelation 1:6). Only Jesus testifies to what is true and does what has to be done allowing Himself to be taken to the cross. Only Jesus is **faithful**. He had been faithful in prayer.

# Chapter 42

## Jesus' Late-night Trial

(Luke 22:54–65)

At this point in our story, the various legal trials of Jesus begin. Luke 22:54–65 describes some kind of night-time trial. There are at least five trials altogether. (i) Jesus was questioned late at night on Thursday evening in the house that belonged to Annas and his relative Caiaphas. (ii) Then He was tried again on the Saturday morning before the Sanhedrin, the Jewish parliament. (iii) He was sent to Pilate. (iv) Pilate sent Him to Herod. (v) From Herod He came back to Pilate again.

The idea put forward by some scholars that Luke records only a daytime trial is not right. There is no hint of a time-gap between the late-night arrest and the interrogation. The fire of 22:56 implies a cold night. The passing of an hour's time in 22:59 and the later coming of the day (22:66) all indicate that this passage records a night-time interrogation.

1. **Jesus faced unfair accusers**. Jesus' enemies were unfair. Of course! When people are showing enmity, they do not bother about justice or fairness. There were at least two things about this trial that were irregular, if not illegal. It was surely wrong to accuse Jesus in a night-time trial. Later on in Israel's history (and perhaps even at this stage) it would be illegal to do so. And it was highly irregular for the Sanhedrin to be interrogating Jesus in a private house.

2. **Jesus was burdened with weak followers**. One of the twelve had betrayed Him. Ten had fled and left Him to His fate. Only Peter showed any loyalty and soon his weakness would be revealed. Jesus wanted His disciples to stand with Him, even if it caused them suffering and death. He had just commended them for staying with Him amidst His troubles (see 22:28).

134

They had shown loyalty so far but now they refused to identify with Jesus. Jesus wants us to identify with Him and His cause. Peter is an example of a believer who fails to confess Christ in a situation in which he is being tested. There are four steps to his fall into denying Jesus.

He followed Jesus at a distance (22:54). He did not want to disown Jesus altogether and was deeply concerned to know what would happen. Yet he would not boldly stand by Jesus and suffer with Him if necessary.

He was pretending to be unrelated to Jesus (22:55–57). The servant girl realised that he had some connection with Jesus, but he did not want his faith to be known at precisely this time.

He turned down an opportunity when challenged. He was given a chance to identify with Jesus but, not only did he not voluntarily witness to his faith, even when it was almost forced upon him he avoided the challenge. Again and again opportunities came to him (22:58–60) but he did not want them. Then the cock crowed (22:60b), and with a look Jesus reminded Peter of their earlier conversation (22:61). Peter was overwhelmed with distress. He **is** a believer. His faith has stumbled but has not ceased to exist. Jesus prayed for his continuing faith. We have seen what led to Peter's fall: (i) over-confidence, (ii) prayerlessness, (iii) indecision, (iv) foolish company.

**But what about Jesus?** All along He has been listening to the conversation. He has been mindful of Peter even when Peter was denying Him. For the rest of the night Jesus was alone. He was suffering in our place, bearing the shame and the guilt of our sin. Jesus had to suffer. When people suffer together, they become very close to each other. One reason why Jesus suffered so much is so that He might be drawn close to us in our sufferings. Consider His sufferings here.

1. **He suffered violence** (22:63). Some people fear violence more than others. Some like a fight! They make good soldiers. These tough Roman soldiers thought it was fun to beat up Jesus. Other people hate the slightest hint of violence and shrink from it – even on a TV programme. Certainly Jesus would have hated it. To enjoy violence for its own sake was

bad enough but to be doing it in the courts of Jerusalem was hateful.

2. **He endured the distress of not having His ministry taken seriously** (22:64). They blindfolded Him and then asked for a display of His supernatural knowledge. What would they have done, we wonder, if He had given them what they asked for? Would they have charged entrance fees to watch Him perform?

3. **He suffered insult** (22:64). They ridiculed His famous ability to prophesy and speak for God. As we see the greatness of Jesus in His willingness to endure terrible adversity, so we see too the disgusting cruelty of human beings towards each other. It was bad enough that they arrested the Son of God, but now they added insult to injury, piling blasphemy upon blasphemy. Yet this is the very reason why the Son of God is going to the cross. Jesus is having to die because men and women are *'foolish, disobedient, serving various lusts and pleasures, living in malice and envy, hateful and hating one another'* (Titus 3:3). We see it all in these events leading up to the cross of our Lord Jesus Christ.

But Jesus showed calmness and restraint in the midst of everything that was happening to Him. What an example He is to us! It should lead us into refusing all complaint and irritation of spirit when some relatively small vexations are put upon us or when the world throws its insults at us. Jesus went through the worst kind of insult and provocation and yet stayed cool. We His disciples must learn to be like Him.

# Chapter 43

## Facing Prejudice
### (Luke 22:66–71)

Jesus is kept awake all night. He must have been physically exhausted when they took Him to the 'Sanhedrin', the Jewish parliament, at daybreak, on what we would call Friday morning (22:66). The entire parliament is there. Everyone has arrived early. The authorities are eager to get rid of Jesus as speedily as they can, so they are willing to call a session of parliament very early in the morning. *'If you are the Christ, tell us,'* they say (22:67).

As we look at the last hours of Jesus' ministry here on earth, we see many aspects of His sufferings. Jesus had to suffer. One reason why He suffered so much is so that He might be drawn close to us in our sufferings. Anything we might suffer He knows about. He has been through the equivalent of every trouble we might face.

Our story here is a classic picture of prejudice. Prejudice is when you are so hostile to someone or to a group of people that before you know the facts about them you have already made up your mind. Jesus went through a second trial on the Friday morning in the presence of the 'Sanhedrin', the Jewish parliament. Jesus' sufferings here help us when we face prejudice, for no one ever faced prejudice as severe and wicked as what we see here.

1. **Prejudice is when a person's mind is made up without considering the facts**. We see it here. These religious leaders are not holding a trial in order to find out anything. They have already got fixed and determined opinions about Jesus. They are simply rushing through a trial because there is no other way of getting rid of Him. But they are already thoroughly

convinced that they have to get rid of Him. This is what prejudice is: having one's mind so closed that it is quite impossible to reconsider.

2. **Prejudice is not affected by intelligence**. These people who are acting as the judges of Jesus are, one might think, reasonably intelligent people. They hold official positions. They are elders, chief priests, scribes. You would think that these people would be capable of making an intelligent judgement. Yet they are utterly gripped with prejudice. Actually what controls these people is not their intelligence but their blind animosity towards Jesus. Animosity stops you from thinking intelligently. It knocks out of action your ability to consider the facts properly. It fills you with blind hostile emotion which makes you totally incapable of judging fairly.

3. **Prejudice leads to unfairness**. How unjust these men are towards Jesus. We have already seen two highly irregular aspects to their procedure. (i) It was wrong to accuse Jesus in a night-time trial. (ii) It was highly irregular for the Sanhedrin to be interrogating Jesus in a private house. But there is more. (iii) They try to get Jesus to incriminate Himself. *'If you are the Christ, tell us,'* they say (22:67). And (iv) they decide a verdict of guilty immediately, but, in a matter as important as this, a delay of at least one day should take place before the final sentence is made. But all this is brushed aside. They want Him to say something that will get Him into trouble, and will justify them in sentencing Him to death. They are not calmly considering anything.

4. **Jesus questions their objectivity** (22:67). *'You will not believe at all, even if I tell you,'* He says. They have made up their mind in advance. No genuine consideration of Jesus' claims takes place. No questions are allowed to disturb their refusal to think! *'You will not answer me if I ask you anything'* (22:68). There is no discussion or any attempt to find out the truth. They do not want to know the truth.

5. **But Jesus answers their question** (22:69). *'From now on'* – beginning any moment now – *'the Son of Man will sit at the right hand of God in the place of power.'* It is a reference to Daniel 7:13. In His death, resurrection and exaltation to

glory, Jesus is just about to be enthroned as the King of the universe. Within one generation Jerusalem will be destroyed. This is very clear talk. They are getting what they want – something to use to get Jesus executed! And Jesus is giving it to them. He is a faithful witness no matter what it will cost Him. He is the very opposite of Peter. They all shout at Him. 'Then you claim that you are God's Son?' they say. 'Yes!' says Jesus. 'You are right!' They don't need witnesses. Jesus will tell them the truth about Himself, regardless of what it costs Him.

What delivers you from prejudice? Nothing but an intervention from God. Paul was in blind prejudice 'breathing out threats and slaughter against the disciples of the Lord' when Jesus stepped dramatically into his life and turned him around (Acts 9:1ff.). The only thing that will deliver us is an intervention in our life that turns us around. Are you suffering because of someone who is viewing you with extreme prejudice? Do you have an enemy who constantly jumps to false conclusions about you – long before he or she knows what the facts are. And he is not very interested in knowing the facts anyway. He or she has already made up their minds. You can know that Jesus was treated in exactly the same way. There is a more painful question: are you treating anyone in this way? If you really want to know, Jesus will tell you the truth – but are you open to His voice?

# Chapter 44

# A Surprising Friendship

(Luke 23:1–12)

Let us try to get a picture of what is happening at this stage of Jesus' sufferings. Jesus is now taken to Pilate (Matthew 27:1–2; Mark15:1; Luke 23:1; John 18:28). Matthew records Judas' suicide (Matthew 27:3–10). Jesus is tried before Pilate (Matthew 27:11–14; Mark 15:2–5; Luke 23:2–5; John 18:29–38). Then He is sent to Herod (Luke 23:6–12). Pontius Pilate was the sixth of the various 'procurators' ruling Judea on behalf of the Roman empire. He did not normally stay in Jerusalem but was there to keep order during the Passover season. Now the Jewish leaders come to Pilate with a whole string of accusations against Jesus. They accuse Jesus of being a dangerous enemy of the state, of refusing to pay taxes, of assuming the title 'king' (23:1–2). Pilate takes Jesus into the palace of Herod where he is staying (as John's Gospel tells us) and enquires more closely into Jesus' claims. *'Are you the King of the Jews?'* he asks (23:3). Jesus says 'Yes', but Pilate knows that this is not a political claim and is no threat to his political career. *'I find no fault in this man,'* he says (23:4).

Pilate faces the question that everyone has to face: what will you do with Jesus? What will you do when Jesus is standing before you and you are interviewing Him (or is He interviewing you?) and you have to make a decision about Him. What will you do when you have a strong conviction that something you are involved in is not right and yet you are in the presence of Jesus. What happened to Pontius Pilate literally and physically often happens to us in our spiritual experience.

1. **Pilate finds himself unexpectedly challenged with a decision he has to make about Jesus**. He did not normally

140

spend time in Jerusalem; his headquarters were at Caesarea. He hated the Jews and often was quite violent towards them. He spent his time in the theatres, at the Roman baths, watching athletics and games, and enjoying the 'high society' that was part of his life as a leading military figure. Suddenly he is brought face to face with Jesus and he has to make a decision. What will he do with Jesus?

2. **He tries to make a right decision** (23:4). *'I find no fault in him,'* he says to the Jewish leaders. He wants to do the right thing if he can.

3. **He finds himself coming under pressure** (23:5). The Jewish leaders will not easily give up. Pilate finds himself pressurised to do something he knows is unjust.

4. **He tries to pass the responsibility to someone else** (23:6–12). Jesus is a Galilean, and Herod is the ruler of Galilee. Now Pilate thinks he has a way out. He will pass the responsibility to Herod Antipas. But it can be surprisingly difficult to push aside a challenge which comes from the presence of Jesus.

**So Herod also finds himself face to face with Jesus**. Herod's story is totally different. This Herod Antipas, a son of Herod the Great whom we know from Matthew 2, was a vain and wicked man, who was guilty of many sins and crimes (see Mark 8:15; Luke 3:19; 13:31, 32). He had beheaded John the Baptist (Matthew 14:1–12) when John criticised him for marrying the wife of his half-brother Philip. Now Herod is also confronted with Jesus. Pilate had never wanted to see Jesus; Herod had often wanted to see Him. Jesus has a lot to say to Pilate, but nothing to say to Herod. There is one thing worse than being confronted with a decision, and that is not being confronted with a decision because Jesus will not speak to you.

1. **Herod is interested in the supernatural**. He has heard about Jesus' miracles and is interested in seeing miracles. Who isn't? But being interested in miracles is not the same as being interested in being reconciled to God.

2. **He is interested in preaching and religious discussion**. We remember how he liked to hear the preaching of John the Baptist.

3. **But God's voice had ceased to come to him**. Why should God speak to us if we will not heed what He has already said? God had often spoken to Herod Antipas. John the Baptist had told Herod all that he needed to hear. But Herod would never listen to John. So why should Jesus say anything more to him? Those who will not hear God's voice will find that He ceases to speak.

4. **Herod confirms his own rejection**. He makes his rejection sure by intensifying his hatred of God. He has plenty of interest in religion, but no interest in changing his ways.

The two men become friends. Jesus either brings people together because they love Him or He brings them together because they reject Him. People only become friends if they have something in common. What Pilate and Herod had in common was that they both found a way to reject Jesus. When God's judgement day comes people will not be able to plead that they had no chance to hear God's voice. All sorts of people are confronted with Jesus. Some are like Pilate. They are totally ignorant, but Jesus is willing speak to them. The question is: what will they do when Jesus tell them about the kind of King that He is?

Others have heard God's voice in the past, but judgement day has already come for them. There is no point in talking to them any further. They go on living in this world but God has finished with them. The very presence of Jesus could do little for Pilate and nothing for Herod. The question is: what will we do with Jesus when we hear His voice?

# Chapter 45

## Insincerity
(Luke 23:13–25)

Almost everyone in the story of Jesus' trial and condemnation is guilty of extreme insincerity. There are few people who are willing to see the truth, stand by the truth and act on the truth.

Jesus is brought back to Pilate again. Pilate declares Him innocent (23:13–16) and offers to release Jesus or Barabbas (Matthew 27:15–23; Mark 15:6–14; Luke 23:17–23; John 18:39–40). He scourges Him (John 19:1–15) and finally releases Him to be crucified (Matthew 27:24–26; Mark 15:15; Luke 23:24–25; John 19:16).

1. **Pilate displays great insincerity.** He tells the Jewish authorities that he could find no reason to accuse Him of any crime (23:13–14). Most of the observers of Jesus at this time mention His purity. Pilate emphasises Jesus' innocence. Herod was hostile but had no charge to make against Him (23:15). Peter who witnessed the early stages of these events said Jesus 'committed no sin' (1 Peter 2:22). The soldier who observed Jesus said, *'This man was innocent'* (23:47). Jesus as the sacrifice for our sins had to be a 'lamb without blemish', like most of the sacrifices of the Mosaic law. One sinner could not die for another sinner. Only a sinless Saviour could help us. God let Jesus' enemies thoroughly examine Him. None of them had any charge against Jesus that could stand up to examination.

But it all goes to show Pilate's great insincerity. Despite his knowledge that Jesus is innocent of any crime, Pilate shows his weakness and injustice. Perhaps more than anyone in the history of the world, Pilate is famous for making an unjust

143

decision. The decision came upon him suddenly. He wanted to make a right decision, but had no strength of character to withstand the pressure of the Jewish leaders. He had tried to pass the responsibility to someone else, but the attempt had not succeeded. Now he shows his unwillingness to sincerely do the work that he is given authority to do. Pilate tries compromise. *'I will punish him and release him'* (23:16). He has just pronounced that Jesus is innocent yet still says, 'I will punish him'. He is already going against what he knows is right. He knows Jesus is innocent but Pilate is under pressure to have Him murdered within the framework of the law! Yet he would rather not go all the way with his wickedness. He will compromise if he can, and punish Jesus. He hopes to please the Jews and does not regard it as greatly wicked to punish an innocent man.

2. **The Jewish leaders show great insincerity**. With one voice the people demand that Jesus should be crucified. The word 'they' in 23:18 means the people generally. Luke's Gospel was not the first account of these events, and he assumes that we know about Barabbas and the way the Jewish leaders persuaded the common people to demand Jesus' death. (Verse 17 is omitted by the best manuscripts. It was not in the original text but was added by early scribes because of Matthew 27:15 and Mark 15:6.)

Pilate thinks he has another way of avoiding a decision against Jesus. He can pronounce Jesus guilty as the Jews wish but then set Him free in accordance with the custom of releasing a prisoner at Passover time. But that does not please the Jewish leaders either. It again shows the insincerity of Jesus' enemies. They all know Barabbas is guilty. He is a bloodthirsty revolutionary (23:19). Pilate appeals to them a second time (23:20), but the Jewish leaders and the people of Jerusalem prefer to see a murderer released and someone who claims to be a Messiah executed (23:21). Pilate's third attempt (23:22) meets with no success (23:23).

So it is all wilful and yet blind hatred of Jesus. This is the essence of the human problem. Here we have a very clear picture of human sinfulness. Sin is hatred of the righteousness of God. Why should Jesus face such opposition and hatred?

He healed people. He forgave people in the name of God. He changed the lives of hardened and wicked sinners. He brought people like Levi the tax collector from his corrupt work for the pagan Romans to faith in the God of Israel. He brought Zacchaeus to return the profits he had swindled plus 300 per cent. Why should anyone want to be so cruel and unjust as to crucify Jesus?

But this is what sin is like. Sin is blind and ignorant animosity towards God. Men and women rebel against God. They have an entirely wrong attitude to Him. Although deep within us all there is some kind of sense of justice, yet it is all abandoned when it comes to the way in which we treat God and His Son. Somehow we feel threatened by Jesus even when His greatest desire is to save us. These ignorant and wicked men are blindly hating Jesus while He is in the very process of going to the cross to be the Saviour of their sins. However, it is pleasant to recall that a few weeks later – on the Day of Pentecost – many of those who had cried 'Crucify Him!' would be brought to distress by Peter's preaching and would find forgiveness and salvation.

Pilate gives in to the Jewish demands (23:24). The guilty man is released; the innocent Saviour is crucified. Barabbas is of course a picture of what happens to all of us who put our faith in Jesus. Even to the Pilates and the Caiaphases of this world salvation is offered. There is no truth in their mouth; their heart is destruction (Psalm 5:9) – but the Saviour dies for those who have made a wrong decision, those who have shown great insincerity. We who are guilty men and women are released, because Jesus the innocent Saviour is crucified instead of us.

# Chapter 46

# The Cross of Christ

(Luke 23:26–56a)

Jesus is mocked by the soldiers (Matthew 27:27–31a; Mark 15:16–20a) and then is led away to Golgotha (Matthew 27:31b–32; Mark 15:20b–21; Luke 23:26–32; John 19:17a), where He is crucified (Matthew 27:33–37; Mark15:22–26; Luke 23:33–34; John 19:17b–27). Jesus is ridiculed on the cross (Matthew 27:38–43; Mark15:27–32a; Luke 23:35–38). Others who are being crucified are near Him (Matthew 27:44; Mark 15:32b; Luke 23:39–43). Jesus dies (Matthew 27:45–54; Mark 15:33–39; Luke 23:44–48; John 19:28–30); His death is witnessed by some of the women who have been loyal to Him (Matthew 27:55–56; Mark 15:40–41; Luke 23:49). After His death Jesus' side is pierced with a spear (John 19:31–37) to ensure that He is truly dead. He is buried in a rich man's tomb (Matthew 27:57–61; Mark 15:42–47; Luke 23:50–56; John 19:38–42). Let us ponder the six matters that Luke records.

1. **Jesus is led away to Golgotha** (23:26–32). A Cyrenian Jew was made to carry Jesus' cross (23:26). What an experience! It led to Simon's conversion and decades later one of his children was a Christian living in Rome (for Mark 15:21 was written for Christians in Rome; compare Romans 16:13). Simon found that the day he came to Jerusalem from North Africa would be the day when his entire life was changed for him and his family.

There are women who are moved at Jesus' sufferings (23:27) but within fifty years the people of Jerusalem will themselves suffer terribly as Jerusalem is destroyed and removed from having any special significance in the purposes of God. God delights in mercy, but the city of Jerusalem would suffer judgement for its rejection of Jesus. Jesus tells the women to weep for themselves (23:28–30). *'If men do these things when the tree is green* [and does not burn easily] *what will happen when it is dry* [and therefore is easily able to be burned]' (23:31). It means: If this is what happens to innocent Jesus, what kind of calamity will come upon wicked Jerusalem?

2. **Jesus is crucified** (23:33–34). There were probably many men who were crucified at the same time as Jesus. Two of them are of special interest (23:33). It was prophesied about Jesus that He would be a Saviour who was *'numbered with the transgressors'* (Isaiah 53:12). Jesus prays for those who are treating Him with such amazing cruelty and injustice (23:34; on the Day of Pentecost the prayer was answered for in the crowds of that day were many of the same people who had not long before been in Jerusalem for Passover).

3. **Jesus experiences terrible shame on the cross** (23:35–38). The people admit that He saved others! They also see that He does not save Himself. Exactly. He saves people by not saving Himself from the cross. They were right at every point, but could not believe what they were witnessing. The people, the rulers, the soldiers, even the criminals, all ridicule Jesus. Jesus hangs naked in unimaginably ghastly shame. He could not explain to anyone what was happening. Nothing but *'the joy set before him'* enabled him to *'endure the cross, despising the shame'* (Hebrews 12:2).

4. **Others who are being crucified are near Him** (23:39–43). In the midst of everything, Jesus is still saving sinners. One of the thieves realises his sin, recognises a Saviour in the crucified Jesus (having faith despite all the squalor and disgrace of the cross) and prays in faith to Jesus! Jesus gives him an assurance of heaven that very day. The thief had not had much time to be very religious or do many good deeds. He had not been baptised. He had not done much reading of the Bible lately. I can't imagine when he last went to the synagogue. But a few seconds of faith gave him salvation! One writer I know does not like us getting our theology from 'the thief on the cross'. I am not surprised. Not everyone likes the gospel, and the 'thief on the cross' is such a clear presentation of the gospel message.

5. **Jesus dies** (23:44–49). Two things happen as Jesus dies. Darkness comes over the whole land, for three hours, as the shining of the sun was miraculously obscured (23:44–45a). The very universe expressed its displeasure as the sins of the world were laid on Jesus. God abandoned Him. Human beings abandoned Him. Even the sun abandoned Him. The sins of the world were laid on Jesus and He was plunged into the deepest experience of the anger of God against sin. Yet at the same time the curtain of the temple is torn into two. It expresses the fact that the atoning death of Jesus has opened a way into closer fellowship with God than has ever been possible before! Jesus' work is done! Jesus hands over His life to the powers of death. Immediately there is the feeling among the witnesses that something immense has happened. A soldier is instantly convinced of Jesus' genuineness (23:47). The crowds are instantly convinced that they have assisted in something that was deeply wicked and yet deeply meaningful (23:48). The women who have been loyal to Jesus witness His death and stay there for a long time, so great is the feeling that something immense has just happened (23:49).

6. **After His death Jesus is buried in a rich man's tomb** (23:50–56a). Everything happens in such a way that there can be not the slightest doubt that Jesus was dead and buried. When He is raised less than forty-eight hours later, it will be difficult to deny that He was genuinely dead and buried. The fact of Jesus' death could hardly be more certain – but that in itself will mean that the fact of Jesus' resurrection will be certain for those who are not so prejudiced that it blinds their eyes to the truth. The Saviour has died for the sins of the world. But the resurrection is not far away!

# Chapter 47

## Jesus Alive from the Dead!
### (Luke 23:56b–24:12)

The last phrase of Luke 23:56 tells us that the women who had witnessed Jesus' death rested on the next day, which was the Saturday Sabbath. What would everyone have been thinking about on this day? The Mosaic law forbade much moving about or travelling. Everyone would have stayed where they were.

The next day the women make their way to the tomb (see Matthew 28:1–8; Mark 16:1–8; Luke 24:1–12; John 20:1–13). It is very early in the morning. They leave before dawn and dawn breaks as they are going to the tomb (24:1a). They were planning to anoint the body of Jesus (24:1b) but when they get to the tomb the stone is rolled away (24:2) and the body of the Lord Jesus is not there (24:3; for the first time Jesus is called 'the Lord Jesus').

**Here is a crucial fact of history**. On Friday night Jesus was dead and buried. On Sunday morning Jesus' tomb was empty. The Jewish authorities certainly did not have the body of Jesus (for they would gladly have produced it to show that He was dead). The same documents that tell us that Jesus was dead and buried also tell us that within forty-eight hours the tomb was empty. Nothing in our story so far gives us any reason to think the disciples had the body. So what happened to the body of Jesus? Jesus was raised from the dead! It would have been impossible for the disciples to have preached the resurrection so soon after Jesus' death if they had known that it was not true. They were willing to suffer terrible persecution when their enemies got angry about the preaching of Jesus' resurrection. Why suffer persecution for something that is not true? The willingness of the early Christians even to die for their faith was because they knew that it was a sheer fact that Jesus had been raised from the dead.

What other explanation is possible? If the Jews had the body they would have produced it. If the disciples stole the body it is hard to believe that they would endure such persecution and show such heroism for preaching something they knew was untrue. Why preach an untruth when it will only bring suffering? The disciples could hardly have been imagining Jesus to be alive when He was not. They were not expecting Jesus to be alive; they were slow to believe the story the women told them. All explanations fail except one: Jesus really was raised from the dead.

At the tomb-site Jesus appears to them (Matthew 28:9–10) but the guards spread a false report (Matthew 28:11–15). Jesus appears specially to Mary (John 20:14–18), to the men on the road to Emmaus (Luke 24:13–35), to the disciples (Luke 24:36–43; John 20:19–23) and to the disciples with Thomas (John 20:24–29). Matthew records the great commission (Matthew 28:16–20). Luke records the ascension (Luke 24:44–53). John records Jesus' appearing to the disciples by the sea of Tiberias and His recommissioning of Peter (John 21:1–25).

In Luke's story two angels appear to the women (24:4) and announce that Jesus is no longer to be found among the corpses of the dead (24:5). They should have believed all along that He would be raised from the dead because He had spoken about it to the disciples (24:6–7). With this angelic reminder the women remember that Jesus had indeed spoken of resurrection (24:8). They immediately go back to where the disciples are staying – in a house in Jerusalem – and tell them the news (24:9). Luke mentions three women who had the privilege of being the first to know that Jesus was alive: Mary Magdalene, Joanna, the other Mary (mother of James one of the apostles). And there were other women at the tomb as well (24:10). The men can hardly credit what they say (24:11), but Peter runs to the tomb and finds that it is true (24:12).

Jesus is alive! Death is not the end of human life. **There is life beyond the grave**. Jesus proves it; He has died and returned to life. Jesus has power over death. No one takes His life from Him. He lays it down willingly, and He has power to take it again (John 10:17, 18). His sinlessness enables Him to take His life again.

**The resurrection proves the claims of Jesus**. Constantly people asked Jesus for a sign that would prove He was who He claimed to be. You would have thought that His many miracles were enough, but they wanted more! Jesus told them that no sign would be given except the sign of the prophet Jonah – the resurrection (11:16, 29–30; see also John 2:18–22).

**The resurrection of Jesus is the cause in some way of the resurrection of the entire human race**. Jesus is the resurrection and the life (John 11:25). In Christ all of the human race will be physically made alive. This does not mean that all will inherit salvation, but all will rise to give an account of the deeds done in the body.

**The Christian is raised with Christ**. The same resurrection-power that was used when Jesus took His life again is the power that is at work in the Christian. When a person believes in Jesus, he or she is joined on to the resurrection-power of Jesus. Christ is totally victorious over death. Paul says, *'Since Christ was raised from the dead, he cannot die again. Death no longer has dominion over him'* (Romans 6:10). Then he adds, *'Reckon yourselves to have died to sin, and reckon you are people who are alive to God in Christ Jesus'* (6:11). The resurrection power of Jesus is already at work in every Christian. The Bible tells us to believe and live confidently and boldly for God.

# Chapter 48

## The Emmaus Road

(Luke 24:13–35)

We meet two disciples who are very depressed. It is the day of Jesus' resurrection but they do not know it. They are utterly miserable and discouraged.

1. **Disciples who have no grasp of the resurrection of Jesus will find themselves utterly discouraged**. This is the way it is with these two men. They are disciples, and Jesus is alive! But they have not yet realised that Jesus is alive. Their discouragement shows itself in two ways. It shows itself in their appearance. Their faces are downcast. Anyone looking at them can see they are utterly depressed.

It shows itself in their talking. They walk eleven kilometres, talking about the failure of all of their hopes. They 'talk and discuss' all the way. When Jesus draws near they want to tell out the whole story to Him as well.

People who are depressed either talk too little – running away and hiding themselves – or they talk too much, going over and over what has happened, but without coming to any encouraging conclusions. These men have done eleven kilometres of walking and talking but they are still discouraged!

2. **The remedy to discouragement is to discover that Jesus is alive**! Jesus helps them out of their distress and discouragement.

First of all, He rebukes them. How foolish they are. How slow and sluggish to read and grasp hold of God's Word. We must notice that Jesus does not say, 'But I am Jesus! Here I am. I am alive!' He talks to them about the resurrection in the Scriptures. If they had been more eager and attentive to their Old Testament Scriptures they would not be so discouraged.

The Old Testament is full of descriptions of a suffering Messiah who subsequently would be crowned with glory and honour. If they had paid more attention to the Scriptures they would not have been so surprised about the death of Jesus, and they would not have been so sceptical about the women who were telling them that Jesus was alive. Their problem was slowness of heart. They did not have sufficient spiritual eagerness to search the Scriptures looking for the truth of God.

After Jesus has shown them His resurrection in one way, He shows them His resurrection in another way. He repeats what He had done in the Lord's Supper three days earlier. Immediately their eyes are opened and they realise that Jesus is indeed alive from the dead. Once they have seen the resurrection in the Scriptures, Jesus is ready to show them in another way that He is indeed alive.

This is the way it will be with us. God wants us to believe His Scriptures. Jesus is indeed alive. Once we have come to see by sheer faith that Jesus is alive, then there will be other ways in which we experience His resurrection power.

We must notice exactly what the disciples said. *'Did not our hearts burn within us when He opened to us the Scriptures?'* What made their hearts 'burn' was not the moment when they realised they were talking to the risen Lord Jesus Christ. Their hearts were burning even before that time. Their hearts started burning when they saw the resurrected Lord Jesus Christ in the pages of the Old Testament. They experienced Jesus in the Scriptures before they realised to whom they were talking.

We shall never in this life meet with Jesus in His physical resurrection body. Jesus has ascended into heaven and I do not think anyone ever meets Him in His resurrection body. Not just yet. We shall meet Him in that way – but only after this life. We have to meet with Jesus in the way that the Emmaus Road disciples first met with Him. They saw through the Scriptures and by the Holy Spirit that Jesus is alive. Then Jesus did something that confirmed their faith. They had to have faith in the Scriptures first; then their faith was confirmed. That is the way it will be with us. Through the witness of the Scriptures we know that Jesus is alive. We talk to Him through our faith in His resurrection. He talks to us by the Holy Spirit and our hearts burn within us.

What a difference there is between the beginning and the end of this story. They begin with a slow heart. They end up with a burning heart. They begin with scepticism concerning the reports they have had from the women. They return full of faith. They had walked eleven kilometres from the place where they had heard about the women seeing Jesus, and they were full of depression all the way. Now they return full of faith and joy. They walked eleven kilometres with depressed faces. They go back eleven kilometres all the way to Jerusalem, radiant with joy. They have met with the risen Lord Jesus Christ. But remember they met with the risen Jesus first in the Scriptures. Their hearts started burning within them as Jesus read the Scriptures to them.

Jesus is to be found all over the Old Testament. Jesus began with Moses, and then He went on to the prophets, and to the rest of the Scriptures. He went through the entire Old Testament showing that these Scriptures were all about Him. What a Bible study that was! The Holy Spirit was present in power and the greatest expositor of the Scripture that there ever was was present with them. This is the way to read the Bible – with Jesus by our side. It can still happen by the Holy Spirit. And when it does our hearts will once again burn within us.

## Chapter 49

# The Reality of Resurrection
### (Luke 24:36–43)

There are at least two kinds of knowledge, and two ways of knowing things. You can know things by observation, and you can know things by faith in what God says. The two kinds of knowledge are quite different. When Jesus rose from the dead and first appeared to His disciples, He rebuked them for not believing in His resurrection before they saw Him with their own eyes. Jesus wanted them first to believe in resurrection without it being proved to them. He wanted them to know the resurrection first by faith in the Old Testament Scriptures and only second by seeing Him with their very eyes. The apostle John came to believe in the resurrection before he actually saw the risen Lord Jesus Christ (see John 20:8–9). The disciples on the road to Emmaus saw it in the Scriptures before they realised that they were seeing the risen Lord. Jesus wanted His disciples to be thoroughly convinced in both ways that He was alive from the dead. Every Christian has to see in the Scriptures that He is the resurrected Lord Jesus Christ. And part of His plan was that there would also be a group of apostles who would be 'eye-witnesses of the resurrection' (Acts 1:22; see also 1 Corinthians 9:1). Luke 24:36–43 is about knowing the historical facts through having witnessed them visibly and tangibly. Luke 24:44–48 refers to their understanding the resurrection through the Scriptures. Luke 24:49–52 refers to the Spirit's sealing both their historical knowledge and their knowledge of the Scriptures.

**The resurrected Lord Jesus Christ was full of graciousness**. Luke 24:36 records the first occasion when Jesus appeared to the ten disciples. Thomas was absent, and Judas was no longer alive. Suddenly Jesus appears to them. These very men had all disowned Jesus and had fled for their lives when He was arrested. Yet despite their weakness of faith and their cowardice there is not a single criticism of them from Jesus. *'Peace be with you,'* He says. Jesus is a gracious Saviour. He has risen from the dead to bring us peace, not to condemn us.

**The resurrection body of Jesus had new powers**. At one point in the story of the two disciples on the road to Emmaus, Jesus disappeared (Luke 24:31). Now Jesus suddenly appears (Luke 24:36; see also John 20:19–23). It seems that the new resurrection body of Jesus was able to pass through closed doors. Nothing like this ever happened during His earthly lifetime. He passed through the grave clothes (John 20:6–9). The body of Jesus had powers after the resurrection that it did not have before.

**He showed them that His new body is really a body**. The new resurrected body of the Lord Jesus Christ is a great mystery. The disciples are startled as if they were seeing a ghost (24:37). Jesus' body has new powers and can pass through doors, yet Jesus wants to make it very clear that it really is a tangible body (24:38–40). He is not a ghost or spirit. His body is not some kind of non-material body. (In passing we note that Jesus distinguishes very clearly between 'spirits' – beings that truly exist but do not have a body – and beings that are not just 'spirits' but they **also** have a body. And 1 Corinthians 15:40 refers to non-living things that have a body but are not 'spirits'.) Jesus' body really is a body. He is not some kind of ghost. He has a **physical** body (24:39). The disciples are overjoyed and can hardly believe what they are seeing, so Jesus takes the trouble to demonstrate the physical nature of His resurrection body (24:41–43).

Jesus shows that He identifies with what He was before His death and resurrection. There is some kind of identity between the pre-resurrection and the post-resurrection body of Jesus. They are able to **recognise the body of Jesus**. When we are first raised from the dead the marks of our previous life are still upon us – at least for a while. The Swiss Reformer John Calvin thought they would then eventually disappear.

What does the resurrection mean to us? (i) It vindicates Jesus. It shows that all along what He was saying and predicting was true. *'These are my words which I spoke to you.'* Jesus' enemies often asked Him to perform a sign to prove that He was the Saviour. On these occasions Jesus would say that no sign would be given them except the sign of the resurrection. Yet Jesus did not appear to His enemies, but only to His disciples. To those who had believed in Him He gave a sign and proof that He was everything He claimed to be – and that proof was the resurrection from the dead. God would surely not raise from the dead a liar and false teacher. Jesus' resurrection was the vindication of His claims. (ii) It shows that resurrection power is available to us. There is such a thing as experiencing the power of Jesus' resurrection (Philippians 3:10). (iii) It is a foretaste of what will one day happen to us, if we do the will of God. He who does the will of God will abide for ever. Believers who live for the Lord Jesus Christ will be raised physically with the same kind of glory that He has, and then they will live for ever. They will be 'raised immortal' (1 Corinthians 15:42). If there were no resurrection of the dead we would be still in our sins. But Jesus is alive from the dead, the first instalment of the raising of all of His people from the dead. It is that certainty which is to make us steadfast, immovable, always abounding in the work of the Lord.

# Chapter 50

## The Forty Days

### (Luke 24:44–53)

After being raised from the dead, Jesus did not go immediately and finally to heaven. There was a very important period of forty days during which He would often appear to His disciples.

1. It was a time when – as we have seen – Jesus **confirmed the reality of His resurrection**.

2. It was a time when Jesus **gave them teaching about interpreting the Old Testament**. We know from Luke 24:44–46 that this was a major point in Jesus' teaching during this period. He opened their minds. This must involve two things. He pointed to the text and showed how it referred to Him. But it is also likely that this 'opening of their minds' included an empowering by the Spirit (we remember John 20:22) which gave them a deeper ability to perceive what is in the Scriptures.

3. Jesus **commissioned them to take the gospel to all nations**. Luke 24:47–48 tells us that they were told to preach repentance and forgiveness to all nations. They would give testimony concerning the literal historical events that had happened in Galilee and in Jerusalem. Luke tells us Jesus stayed with the disciples *'until the day (after giving commands through the Holy Spirit to the apostles whom he had chosen) when he was taken to God'* (Acts 1:2). When He was fulfilling His earthly ministry, Jesus gave commands 'through the Holy Spirit' (Acts 1:2) and via the apostles (Acts 1:2). Soon He will be continuing to give them commands and lead them, only His ruling the church will take place from heaven. During His three-year ministry He spoke by the Holy Spirit. During the

forty days after the resurrection He spoke to them by the Holy Spirit. And after He has ascended He will continue to speak to them by the Holy Spirit. The presence and power of the Holy Spirit will be one of the major themes of the Book of Acts.

3. Jesus **told them about the new experience of the Spirit that they were about to receive** (24:49). They were to stay in Jerusalem until they knew the experience of the Spirit in a deeper way. The forty days was a time when 'the promise of the Father' was held out to His disciples. What is this gift of the Spirit which is deeper than anything known before? There is a giving of the Spirit which is about to come upon them. It is not their conversion or their being brought to faith. The Spirit had already brought them to faith. Judging from Luke 24:49, it is spiritual power which enables bold witness. Judging from Acts 1:8, it is power to witness boldly for Jesus. Judging from Acts 2 it is an abundant sense of the presence of God which leads to overflowing praise and worship.

4. **After Jesus has spent forty days with them He ascends into heaven**. The forty days have been an interim period when the glorified Jesus has been with them. They will never be able to doubt the glory of Jesus, because they had forty days witnessing His resurrection, forty days of preparation for the coming of the Holy Spirit.

**The great dividing line in history is the ascension of Jesus**. Luke writes in Acts 1:2 about *'the day ... when he was taken to God'* (the Greek says 'when he was received'; the idea is 'when He was taken to God'). The resurrection-and-ascension of Jesus Christ was the heavenly enthronement of the man Jesus Christ. The Son of God, who had become a man, was appointed the King of the universe. Luke's Gospel consists of what happened **before** this crucial event of world history. The Book of Acts starts telling the story of what happened **after** this crucial event of world history. The story is not finished yet! The great centrepiece is the resurrection-and-ascension of Jesus. In the ascension, for the first time in the history of the world, a man took over the task of ruling the world. The Son of God was the Son of God before He was born. But He was not a man before He was born. And the man, Jesus Christ, was not King of the universe until the day in history when God *'gave him the name which is above every name'* (Philippians 2:9).

**Jesus moves His headquarters from earth to heaven**. The disciples observe Jesus quite literally ascending into heaven. He ascends into the sky and then disappears from view (24:50–51; Acts 1:9). From now on Jesus will not lead His church by His physical presence with His disciples. Rather He will rule His church from heaven. Jesus will rule His church by pouring the Holy Spirit on the disciples. They will do the work; His power will come upon them from heaven.

Jesus lifts up His hands to pray for them. He leaves the world physically while He is in the position of one praying for blessing. He is in that position still, for He ever lives to make intercession for His church. The disciples worship Him. The resurrection-ascension is the point where they begin worshipping Jesus as God in the flesh.

Jesus leaves His church physically in order to reign and rule over His church in a new way. As He leaves them, He leaves them as a rejoicing and praising people. This is how Jesus wants things to be among His people. Jesus has thoroughly prepared them. They go back to Jerusalem, and begin praising and worshipping God, expecting at any moment the power of the Holy Spirit to fall upon them, as Jesus promised. Soon the promise of the Spirit will come and, by the Spirit, Jesus will continue to lead His church.